Essential Clinical Social Work Series

Series editor: Carol Tosone

For further volumes:
http://www.springer.com/series/8115

Ellen Ruderman • Carol Tosone
Editors

Contemporary Clinical Practice

The Holding Environment Under Assault

Springer

Editors
Ellen Ruderman
Chair, AAPCSW National Study Group
Private Practice
Encino, CA, USA

Carol Tosone
Silver School of Social Work
New York University
New York, NY, USA

ISBN 978-1-4614-4123-6 ISBN 978-1-4614-4124-3 (eBook)
DOI 10.1007/978-1-4614-4124-3
Springer New York Heidelberg Dordrecht London

Library of Congress Control Number: 2012952269

Printed on acid-free paper

Springer is part of Springer Science+Business Media (www.springer.com)

Contents

1 **The World Outside: Its Impact on the Treatment Setting** ... 1
Ellen Ruderman

2 **The Erosion of the Sociopolitical Holding Environment and the Collapse of the Potential Space for Creative Repair** ... 13
Jeffrey Applegate

3 **Grief and Loss in an Age of Global Trauma: Protest and Despair Versus Attachment and Reorganization** ... 19
Judith Kay Nelson

4 **Integrating the Internal and External Worlds of Clinical Social Work: A Philosophical and Political Search** ... 29
Rosalyn Benitez-Bloch

5 **Virtual Intimacy in the Therapeutic Space: Help or Hindrance?** ... 41
Carol Tosone

6 **What Happens to Confidentiality When the Government Enters the Treatment Room via the PATRIOT Act, HIPAA, and Managed Care?** ... 51
Carole Bender

7 **A Perfect Storm: The Influence of Outside Forces on Social Work Education** ... 61
Barbara Berger

8 **Silence in the Clinical Hour: A Time to Speak** ... 73
Billie Lee Violette

9 Real Experiences Revisited: The Significance of Attachment, Separation, and Loss in Adult Psychotherapy 85
Pat Sable

10 Saving the World One Patient at a Time: Psychoanalysis and Social Critique 99
Jennifer Tolleson

Index 117

Contributors

Jeffrey Applegate, Ph.D. School of Social Policy and Social Work, Practice, University of Pennsylvania, Philadelphia, PA, USA

Carole Bender, JD, LCSW UCLA Luskin School of Public Affairs, Department of Social Welfare Center on Child Welfare, Los Angeles, CA, USA

Rosalyn Benitez-Bloch, DSW National Study Group, AAPCSW, Former Faculty, USC and UCLA Schools of Social Work, Los Angeles, CA, USA

Barbara Berger, Ph.D. The Institute for Clinical Social Work, Chicago, IL, USA

Judith Kay Nelson, Ph.D. National Study Group, American Association of Psychoanalysis in Clinical Social Work, The Sanville Institute for Clinical Social Work and Psychotherapy, Berkeley, CA, USA

Ellen Ruderman, Ph.D. Chair, AAPCSW National Study Group, Private Practice of Psychoanalysis and Psychotherapy, Encino, CA, USA

Pat Sable, Ph.D. National Study Group, AAPCSW, USC School of Social Work, Los Angeles, CA, USA

Jennifer Tolleson, Ph.D. Smith College, Institute for Clinical Social Work, Burlington, USA

Carol Tosone, Ph.D. Silver School of Social Work, New York University, New York, NY, USA

Billie Lee Violette, Psy.D. National Study Group, AAPCSW, Psychoanalytic Institute of Northern California, San Francisco, CA, USA

Chapter 1
The World Outside: Its Impact on the Treatment Setting

Ellen Ruderman

In these uncertain times, external events have profoundly altered patients' physical circumstances as well as their emotional states. As therapists, we too are affected by pressuring outside forces—the economy, health care, threats to individuals' rights, war—and we must be aware that our patients bring the same outside world with them when they cross our threshold into the treatment setting. Therefore, as we help patients examine their pasts and their internal states, we must also include examination of the world outside and its effect on their lives. Further, we need to explore the secondary impact of hearing their concerns upon us. We can no longer ignore the elephant in the treatment room.

In 2008, the National Study Group of the American Association of Psychoanalysis in Clinical Social Work (AAPCSW) met in California to address this subject. The exciting discussions that ensued focused on the questions: Shall we, as analysts and therapists, pursue a treatment course based only on theoretical underpinnings, or do we become more attuned to and openly acknowledge the added existential anxiety which also affects our patients' worlds? Is it possible to address the "inner" without also training the therapeutic lens on the "outer?" And can the inner and the outer stand alone, without the therapist becoming more attuned to the "real?"

Following our initial meeting, the AAPCSW National Study Group set to work examining these dilemmas. We concluded that neither therapists nor their patients can ignore the impact of what happens outside the treatment hour. The challenge then becomes how to integrate those external events in our own inner processes, as we work with patients' material and our own countertransference.

The AAPCSW National Study Group's work culminated in a preconference day panel and series of presentations at the AAPCSW conference, "Memory, Myth and Meaning in a Time of Turmoil," held in New York City in February 2009. The panel

E. Ruderman (✉)
Chair, AAPCSW National Study Group, Private Practice, Encino, CA, USA
e-mail: ERuderman@aol.com

E. Ruderman and C. Tosone (eds.), *Contemporary Clinical Practice: The Holding Environment Under Assault*, Essential Clinical Social Work Series,
DOI 10.1007/978-1-4614-4124-3_1, © Springer Science+Business Media New York 2013

and presentations revolved around an earlier published editorial, "The Impact of the Outside World—War, Politics, the Economy, and Healthcare: A Dilemma for Clinical Practice" (Ruderman, 2008).

This book represents the fruition of the AAPCSW National Study Group's efforts and contains chapters contributed by each of the panel's presenters.

The "Isle of Refuge"

The tension between the inner and the outer in psychoanalytic treatment is not new. But the importance of preserving the sanctity of the treatment room has never loomed so large. The treatment setting remains as the isle of refuge for our patients. Yet, there are deep concerns therein.

There is little doubt that the rapid changes and the chaos present in American society have greatly affected and altered the clinical situation. The terrorist attacks on September 11, 2001, produced a generalized and persistent anxiety that now pervades our culture. Perhaps we could call it a collective posttraumatic stress disorder in our populace, which has found its way into the treatment setting and contaminates the serenity of the holding environment.

As clinical practitioners, we can continue to stress the unique qualities of the therapeutic relationship: sensitive exploration, empathic understanding, consistency, and trust. Our patients should still be able to rely on an inviolable confidentiality and consistency in the treatment setting, even though these are no longer dependable commodities in our current world. In addition, if we are able to validate our patients' ongoing concerns and struggles with external impositions, this may go a long way toward reducing their feelings of isolation and ennui.

The AAPCSW National Study Group explored many questions. We challenged ourselves to examine how to maintain our authenticity in the therapeutic encounter while preserving therapeutic neutrality and needed space for the patient's feelings. We asked ourselves: Is therapeutic neutrality really possible and is it in the best interests of our patients? How much, we queried, do we react to patients' discussions of the Iraq and Afghanistan wars, global warming, the economy, and health-care insurance concerns? AAPCSW National Study Group members believe that the enormity of current events—such as financial meltdowns, health-care crises, and ongoing military conflicts—demands that we reconsider whether analysts should maintain a stance of isolation from the turmoil beyond the consulting room. These conflicts, often between theoretical leanings and a new kind of reality, need to be addressed, explored, and discussed.

Two AAPCSW National Study Group authors have written evocative papers whose titles capture the current concerns about the impact of the world entering the treatment room. Applegate (2009) speaks of "The Erosion of the Sociopolitical Holding Environment and the Collapse of the Potential Space for Creative Repair," while Nelson (2009) highlights a theme felt by patients and therapists alike in "Grief and Loss in An Age of Global Trauma: Protest and Despair vs. Attachment and

Reorganization." Each chapter deals with our perceived loss of security and nurturance. Nelson (2009) suggests that if we are able to collectively grieve, instead of switching channels to avoid grotesque images of hunger, poverty, and destruction, we might regain our sense of national harmony and global community.

Despite the focus on reform embodied in a new administration in Washington, patients and therapists alike are confronting multiple upheavals, such as the current economic debacle, the ongoing wars in the Middle East, the years of neglect of education and health-care concerns, and the infringements on civil rights. Closer to home are the grave inequities that deprive large portions of the population from receiving viable physical and mental health care. These are phenomena that, without question, affect the quality of our lives and those of our patients in powerful and personal ways.

Because of their grounding in empathy, trust, and the relationship with the patient, psychoanalytic social workers have much to contribute to our current situation. As is reflected in my earlier works (Ruderman, 1992) on the invaluable role of social work and early social work education on contemporary psychotherapy and psychoanalysis, I have believed for a long time that in the future of modern psychoanalysis, all roads will lead back to social work and its precepts. Benitez-Bloch (2009) further illuminates the important and meaningful contribution of clinical social work to current psychoanalytic theories in her chapter "Integrating the Internal and External Worlds of Clinical Social Work: A Philosophical and Political Search."

Inner and Outer Realities in Transference and Countertransference

Therapists are faced with an exquisite dilemma, which I will illustrate in my discussion later in this work with my patient, Logan. As their patients revisit the past and struggle with current external events that may reactivate past trauma, therapists need to grapple with their own inner processes. How are they to manage and negotiate what is reactivated inside of them? Tosone (2009) so aptly describes the challenges for clinicians working with Skype and other virtual technologies in her chapter "Virtual Intimacy in the Therapeutic Space: Help or Hindrance?" In this book, the AAPCSW National Study Group explores how we deal with countertransference, the real relationship, authenticity, and the concept of mutuality.

Attentiveness to our patients and to our countertransference is essential to analytic treatment. Acknowledging countertransference often helps us to become aware of and focus on the deeper parts of the patient. It also helps us be more in touch with ourselves. Being able to separate one's own feelings as a therapist, deal with our own separations and losses, and be consistently attuned to the needs of our patients is part of the process of helping our patients to grow and to heal. But how do we help our patients to deal with the ever-present tension they carry from the loss of the safety and security they formerly had in a social environment that once felt more caring? Is this not to be a part of our sensitivity and awareness? There is no analytic interpretation that quells the internal anxiety of both patient and analyst when we are dealing with real threat in a society that offers insufficient care.

In a panel entitled "Psychoanalysis in a Chaotic World: Political, Cultural and Ethical Considerations for Analytic Treatment", we focused on countertransference and posited that analysts cannot ignore the impositions from external events on their patients and on themselves. Closing the door to create the sanctity and privacy of the therapeutic treatment setting cannot shut out the threatening and pressured world in which we and our patients live.

While the therapeutic consultation room traditionally has been the soothing "holding environment" where feelings can be explored, processed, and understood, it is also an environment where, as the patient-therapist relationship evolves, patients may learn lessons in trust and authenticity. When patients have to cancel or when they are late for their session and complain about the problems of their work, of longer hours for the same pay, of having to fight for their health care and that the city traffic is strangulating, is it always advisable to interpret their complaints as unconscious resistance? Listening to our own inner processes, we might hear an interior voice saying: "I know just how you feel. Life is more difficult. Tensions are higher. The freeways are like parking lots and something must be done about more equitable health care." We all suffer together. So, together we remain in the session—and the authentic therapist can only be empathic and validating of this reality. Thus, we return to another social work principle: forming an emotional partnership with the patient.

The world has changed drastically and we, as therapists, must adhere even more intensely to Winnicott's dictum of focusing on the inner and outer. The rapidly changing social, cultural, and political landscapes are brought into the treatment situation by our patients, and we must find ways to become more aware of these landscapes and integrate them into our work.

Speaking Out

As therapists, we cannot ignore the world outside of the treatment hour and, moreover, what we do in that world. This brings to mind another focus of the AAPCSW National Study Group, as the chapters in this book will further amplify: encourage therapists and analysts to actively contribute their voices to the public debate. Therapists cannot, by closing the door, shut out what is happening for their patients and for themselves in the world outside. They know, for instance, that the USA PATRIOT Act of 2001 (P.L. 105-107), by its restrictions on individual freedoms of privacy and speech, strikes at the very core of what mental health practitioners and their patients hold most dear. How effective can therapy or analysis be without offering unquestionable assurance of our patients' right to privacy and to confidentiality? The infringements on the civil rights of American citizens imposed by such acts as wire tapping, "no fly" lists, and new forms of racial profiling—especially of those who look Middle Eastern—smack of the worst of the McCarthy Era

(Ruderman, 2010) and its utter disregard for due process of law. Bender (2009) deals with these vital legal issues and how they affect and threaten the sanctity of the treatment situation, in her formidable paper, "What Happens to Confidentiality When the Government Enters the Treatment Room via the PATRIOT Act, HIPPA, and Managed Care?"

Some of us have also become concerned about other trends as they affect therapy practice. As schools of social work across the country eschew analytically focused clinical training in favor of research and evidence-based practice, it may be that we are short-changing trainees who are eager for more psychodynamic understanding of the patients they will be seeing in agencies or in their practices. Dwindling education budgets are also concerning, especially for those of us who remember that our ability to afford graduate schools was due to the NIMH fellowships offered by the federal government. I speak also to the diminishing social and rehabilitative programs in our country and the dwindling budget for education on all levels. These phenomena are illuminated with clarity and grave concern by Berger (2009) in her chapter "A Perfect Storm: The Influence of Outside Forces on Social Work Education."

As clinicians, we must be vigilant to assure that commercialism does not override good clinical education and training and that we include ourselves in the discussion about treatment guidelines. It may be that evidence-based treatment, especially as it centers on short courses of treatment, is not always in the best interests of patients seeking treatment, whether privately, at an agency, or at clinic. We hope that the current attempts at health-care insurance reform will emphasize the well-being of subscribers and not just the profit margins of insurers. But we must join in the debate—our voices need to be heard as well.

Empathy and Economics

There are many ways in which the current economic crises have changed the therapeutic landscape, and the case that follows demonstrates how I have adapted my approach to incorporate this new reality. In my many years in practice, I have never had as many patients who need to talk about the enormous intrusions and incursions assaulting them from the outside. Delaying their usual focus on their present emotional dilemmas and their past disappointments and deprivations, many patients now choose to begin sessions by focusing on economic distress, the political scene, and other existential insecurities and anxieties by which they feel assaulted. While somewhat mystified and saddened by their outside world, they also feel enraged by events over which they feel they have no control. They are also angered by the authorities they designate as responsible, which sets up an interesting shared transference–countertransference phenomena. As therapists and analysts, we represent those who establish boundaries and who represent a unique kind of authority, with these manifestations occurring within the transference; but who then as a citizen does not identify (sometimes strongly) with their patient's plight? Negotiating these feelings within the therapist and attempting to do what is most beneficial for the patient becomes an ongoing challenge, particularly in our current chaotic world.

The following case will serve to illustrate the above-mentioned inequities in our health-care delivery system and the changes they impose on the treatment situation. I have been seeing Melinda, a mental health professional, in individual psychoanalytic psychotherapy. After 3 years in treatment, she finds herself caught in the double bind of falling income and soaring health-care costs. She and her husband, John, now face the loss of their home, and they both feel overwhelmed. Their energies are torn between their enormous concern for their children and the sense of "embattlement" both endure while fighting what they consider to be "totally indifferent and insensitive" (in Melinda's words) outside forces.

To add to her dilemma, her son Gareth, age 9, has juvenile diabetes, and her daughter Samantha, age 7, has severe asthma. Due to the economic downturn, John now must maintain two jobs, while Melinda has to take time off work to take her children to their multiple medical appointments. As both their practices and their salaries have been reduced, they are barely able to afford the costs of their health care. Their insurance company is threatening to cancel their health insurance policy because of what it calls a "preexisting condition." After the sudden untimely death of her brother 4 years ago, Melinda was prescribed an antidepressant medication.

The exigencies of Melinda's situation challenge tried and true approaches to psychoanalytic psychotherapy. Having been trained in a certain manner (at first very classically, and later in relational approaches to psychoanalysis and psychotherapy), I am aware of the concepts of resistance, boundaries, and establishment of the frame. I know the importance of fee setting and the valuing of one's own professional worth in setting the fee and adherence to the time and rented space of the therapeutic hour. However, confronted with modern dilemmas like Melinda's, interpreting the need to change appointments or the request for a reduction of the fee as resistance would be an invalidation of her current reality.

Melinda's besieged plight has required different thinking on my part and, in some circumstances, a more creative way of doing therapy. For example, on two occasions, I have reduced my fees. On other occasions, to better accommodate Melinda's hectic work schedule and commute, I have agreed to her request that we conduct some of her sessions by phone. On several occasions, during a period when Melinda was recuperating from an abdominal surgery and bedridden, her need to maintain the connection to her therapy and her therapist led the two of us to use Skype. This has worked out so well that as John continued to work at two jobs and Melinda was now unable to drive Gareth to his therapy session, Melinda called Gareth's therapist and asked if he could use the same method when she could not get someone to drive Gareth to his sessions. The therapist cooperated, saying that he was "relieved" to be able to do this as it allayed both his and Gareth's worries about Gareth's serious condition.

It was also essential, in Melinda's case, for me to validate her growing concerns about an insurance system that was in need of immediate repair. My validation of her ongoing struggles with external impositions opened for exploration portions of Melinda's childhood during which her shyness and passivity caused her to endure what she called "the silence of my screams," and extraordinary abuse from two older brothers. In one of her recent sessions, she said:

> It wasn't just that you listened and understood. Nor was it that you were able to help me relate so many of my current concerns to a deprived and unhappy childhood. It was your support of my complaints about the unfairness of my HMO that so validated my feelings that it led me to some fruitful protests about their practices directly to them and I think I've really made some headway.

She did, indeed, make headway. She became part of a class-action suit filed by the American Civil Liberties Union against the insurance company which handled her benefits and, in due time, these efforts led to the modification of the "preexistent clause" so that she and John could continue to rely on their benefits for their family.

I have come to believe, as have my colleagues in the AAPCSW National Study Group that empathy, caring, and social responsibility go together. These qualities open the road to social action and can actually, according to some authors, reduce the therapist's sense of helplessness in the countertransference. After becoming involved in a social action group in Berkeley, Aidells and Stern (2003) found that therapists involved in actions aimed at reducing our health-care dilemmas experienced increased empathic connection with their patients. They said: "We have found ourselves living out our own words to clients, about needing to counter isolation and helplessness with connection, action, community, support and conversation with each other" (p. 9).

"All Are Victims"

The impact of the war in Iraq could not have been felt more keenly by therapist and patient as it was in my work with Logan. I had only spent a few sessions with Logan before the following words echoed in my mind: "In war there are no victors and no vanquished, all are victims." I also reflected upon the evocative chapter provided by Violette (2009), "Considerations for Psychoanalytic Treatment in a Time of War," a sober reminder of the exigencies of war and its effect on patients such as Logan.

Logan, 36, had been a master sergeant in the US Army. He is a tall, muscular, soft-spoken, gentle man. His face and chin reveal reddened scar tissue. His demeanor was bent over as he walked into my office unsteadily, struggling to manage with his one remaining arm, a steel crutch. Where his right arm should have been, he had tucked the empty sleeve into his belt.

He had just returned from Iraq after two tours of duty. In between each tour, he was given 4 weeks to return home and spend time with his wife and children. Two weeks before he was due to return from his second tour, he was caught in a surprise attack on his Humvee near Baghdad. Logan lost his right arm and suffered severe contusions to his left eye, leaving him totally blind in that eye. He also lost two of his closest army buddies in the same attack.

After his medical treatment and recuperation, Logan returned home, eager to see his wife of 14 years, Virginia, and his two children Scott, 11, and Bonnie, 8. He was greeted by a note from Virginia tacked to the front door. During our first session, he showed me the note, which read:

> Logan, I'll always love who you were, but you are not the man I married. Your temper tantrums and verbal attacks on me and our kids are too much for me. They are having nightmares, and I am miserable. If and when you get help, maybe we can talk.

Logan was in a state of complete shock and confusion. The shame and humiliation he suffered soon poured out. He felt insufficient as a human being and felt unable to reintegrate himself into what he called "the normal society" which felt to him like "Disneyland." He also spoke of tremendous guilt that he could not save his two best buddies. He experienced severe nightmares and walked around in a sleepless state. His severe posttraumatic stress symptoms had resulted in the threatened loss of those he loved, and a wish to destroy himself rather than, in his words, "go out on the street and be homeless like those guys did when they came back from Nam."

As our work together progressed, he spoke more openly of his shame. It became obvious that these feelings reactivated earlier similar feelings he had as a child. His father, a sergeant in the US Army, would repeatedly call him "sissy boy" for not being able to endure conflict, fighting, or harshness of any kind. He joined the army as a way to prove to his father that, in his words, "I was strong and far from a sissy." Logan also joined up because he wanted to get an education, which he could not afford as a civilian. At the time he was sent to Iraq, he was midway into his studies for electronic engineering. Now, he felt any career was out of the question. "I am too damaged," he said.

While I did not express it, inwardly I was thoroughly outraged by an administration that had deployed young men like Logan to prosecute a war started on false premises. I was more concerned, however, that Logan was ready to turn his own rage inward and upon himself, rather than put responsibility on the societal systems and people within it.

As Logan grew more comfortable with me and began to trust the treatment, he began to ask questions about how I, a person he liked and respected, felt about the war and the politics behind it. I was torn between a wish to be authentic and to disclose my hatred of this war, and all wars in general and a desire to help Logan resolve his internal agonies. To tell him, for example, that I perceive soldiers, male and female, as pawns of political machinations, industrial and economic considerations, of global corporations who profit from wars, and lobbyists who need to sell newly made weapons would be an egregious insult.

I did divulge, however, that I am an active member of two antiwar organizations, and he could not help but notice the necklace I wear upon which "War Is Not Healthy for Children and Other Living Things" is inscribed. On one occasion, when he noticed the necklace, he said, "Well, it certainly wasn't healthy for me or for my family!"

Logan continues in treatment with me and recently requested that I invite Virginia to join us for conjoint sessions. In these sessions, he has attempted to apprise her of his war experience and how it has affected him. He has also begun to hear and understand what Virginia has experienced in seeing and having to live with a completely foreign side of him—a Jekyll and Hyde personality. Further, at my suggestion, he has also joined a group of Iraq vets at his local veterans administration facility. I suggested that group work would be important and very complementary to his individual work.

Psychiatrist Jonathan Shay has argued that group work is essential for veterans and strongly urges them to meet with others who have experienced similar situations and who can appreciate the trauma of war. Shay (1994) asserts:

> The social morality of "what's right," what Homer called Themis is the normal adult's cloak of safety. The trauma narrative of every person with PTSD and character damage is a challenge to the rightness of the social order, to the trustworthiness of Themis. To hear and believe is to feel unsafe. It is to know the fragility of goodness. (p. 193)

In so many of my sessions with Virginia and Logan, their feelings and situations provoked a sense of outrage in me. In exploring my inner process, I also felt a sense of shame. While Logan was losing his entire sense of emotional balance in war's assaultive attack on his mind, how much more could I have done to actively protest an unjust war or the injustice of war in general? What I soon realized was that my feelings of outrage and shame were partly mine, but partly what I was picking up from Logan. I tried to help him get in touch with his own outrage and move away from the self-blaming stance he had assumed for not being "man enough" to return to Iraq and, with regard to Virginia, for not doing "much better" in his married life. There are times when a therapist needs to offer reminders that it is not just the individual that is the focus, but the faulty system in which they reside. This may start in childhood but often evolves to a greedy corporate-industrial society where, as Shay (1994) says, "the betrayal of what is right" is laid at their doorstep. Greenson (1967), and Strean (1998) remind us that there is such a thing as "the real" in a real world, and a real relationship. Not everything is a product of archaic reactivations. Sable's (2009) "Real Experiences Revisited: The Significance of Attachment, Separation and Loss in Adult Psychotherapy" elaborates on the meaningfulness of incorporating the "real" as well as the internal in the treatment situation.

Samuels (1993) speaks of the conflicts that analysts and psychotherapists have when their patients bring overtly political material into the clinical setting and alerts us to the political insensitivity of analysis and psychotherapy to this issue. The AAPCSW National Study Group's contributions in this book offer their own considerations of the impact of the world outside on the treatment situation. How do these concerns affect them and their fellow practitioners? And how can we assess changing clinical perspectives and their effect on the changing roles of analysts and therapists?

Finally, what of the stance of the psychoanalyst or psychotherapist to the intrusions of today's world? In our clinical situations, the above phenomena, the political system that feeds it, as well as our rapidly changing sociocultural-political landscape all impinge upon the sanctity of the treatment situation and pose great challenges for us to explore an expansion not only in our analytic thinking but in our roles as analysts and therapists. Tolleson (2009) in her excellent paper, "Saving the World One Patient at a Time: Psychoanalysis and Social Critique," addresses the paradox of the lack of dissent in psychoanalysis, which, when originally introduced to the world by Freud, was considered a revolutionary movement. As social action chair of our organization, she issues a call for more involvement and action from all clinical practitioners.

In conclusion, the AAPCSW National Study Group is pleased to be part of an endeavor in which we can share our ideas with our colleagues about subjects that we consider to be important matters. We hope to engage with our clinical readers in open, lively, and challenging exchanges about the role of the patient and the analyst during such a critical time in the world. We also hope to keep alive the feeling that as members of the helping profession, we have much to contribute and our voices should be heard. As Dr. Martin Luther King, Jr. said, "Our lives begin to end the day we become silent about things that matter."

Our world and the people in it matter!

References

Aidells, A., & Stern, R. (2003, June). Considerations for clinicians in this time of world upheaval. *California Society for Clinical Social Work Clinical Update*, p. 9.

Applegate, J. (2009, February). *The erosion of the sociopolitical holding environment and the collapse of the potential space for creative repair.* Paper presented at AAPCSW, 11th National Conference, New York, NY.

Bender, C. (2009, February). *What happens to confidentiality when the government enters the treatment room via The Patriot Act, HIPPA, and managed care?* Paper presented at AAPCSW, 11th National Conference, New York, NY.

Benitez-Bloch, R. (2009, February). *Integrating the internal and external worlds of clinical social work: A philosophical and political search.* Paper presented at AAPCSW, 11th National Conference, New York, NY.

Berger, B. (2009, February). *A perfect storm: The influence of outside forces on social work education.* Paper presented at AAPCSW, 11th National Conference, New York. NY.

Greenson, R.R. (1967). The "real" relationship between the patient and the psychoanalyst. In M. Kanzer (Ed.), *The unconscious today* (pp. 213–232), New York, NY: International Universities Press.

Nelson, J. (2009, February). *Grief and loss in an age of global trauma: Protest and despair vs. attachment and reorganization.* Paper presented at AAPCSW, 11th National Conference, New York, NY.

Ruderman, E. (1992). *The vital contribution of social work and early social work education to contemporary psychoanalytic concepts.* Paper presented to California State Society for Clinical Social Work Conference, Monterey, CA.

Ruderman, E. (2002a). Analysts' life experiences and their effects on treatment: Living, learning, and working through. *Psychoanalytic Inquiry, 22*(4), 495–509.

Ruderman, E. (2002b). As time goes by: Life experiences and their effects on analytic technique. *Psychoanalytic Inquiry, 22*(4), 495–509.

Ruderman, E. (2008, June). *Psychoanalysis in a chaotic world: Political, cultural and ethical considerations for analytic treatment. Clinical Social Work Journal*, Vol. 36, No. 2, pp. 216–223, Springer Publishing.

Ruderman, E. (2009, February). *Transformations in the clinical space: The impact of the world outside on treatment.* Paper presented at AAPCSW, 11th National Conference, New York, NY.
Ruderman, E. (2010). *Chasing the red car: Coming of age in the McCarthy Era.* Bloomington, IN: iUniverse.
Sable, P. (2009, February). *Real experiences revisited: The significance of attachment, Separation and loss in adult psychotherapy.* Paper presented at 11th National Conference, New York, NY.
Samuels, S. (1993). *The political psyche.* London, England: Routledge.
Shay, J. (1994). *Achilles in Vietnam: Combat trauma and the undoing of character.* New York, NY: Scribner.
Strean, H. (1998). Resolving some therapeutic impasses by disclosing countertransference. *Clinical Social Work Journal, 27*, 123–140.
Tolleson, J. (2009, February). *Saving the world one patient at a time: Psychoanalysis and social critique.* Paper presented at AAPCSW, 11th National Conference, New York, NY.
Tosone, C. (2009, February). *When the professional is personal: Shared trauma and self-disclosure in the therapeutic relationship.* Paper presented at AAPCSW, 11th National Conference, New York, NY.
USA PATRIOT Act of 2001, P.L. 105–107 (2001); H.Rept. 107–236, pt.1 at 42.
Violette, B. (2009, February). *Considerations for psychoanalytic treatment in a time of war.* Paper presented at AAPCSW, 11th National Conference, New York, NY.

Chapter 2
The Erosion of the Sociopolitical Holding Environment and the Collapse of the Potential Space for Creative Repair

Jeffrey Applegate

The term "holding environment," first coined by the British psychoanalyst Donald Woods Winnicott, has become an established part of the lexicon of mental health professionals representing a wide range of disciplines. The term has a particularly familiar ring for social workers, who grasp intuitively both its manifest meaning and its latent subtleties. We might say this language is, "in our bones," instilled as practice wisdom gleaned from more than a century of work with our most vulnerable and challenged fellow citizens. Jane Addams was establishing holding environments when she began the settlement house movement, and, similarly, the early Charity Organization Societies served crucial "holding" functions for individuals and communities. Across the spectrum of services, from the provision of concrete services to the conduct of psychotherapy, "holding" has always been the relational backdrop of what social workers do in their various roles with individuals, families, groups, and communities (Applegate, 1997).

As elaborated by Winnicott in conjunction with his second wife, social worker Claire Britton Winnicott, the holding environment concept referred both to the biopsychosocial developmental context in which infants are cared for and to the silent, sustaining therapeutic functions essential to effective helping efforts. Winnicott frequently referred to the holding function of social work. He suggested that "casework might be described as the professionalized aspect of the normal function of parents and local units, a 'holding' of persons and of situations, while growth tendencies are given a chance" (Winnicott, 1961, p. 107). Similarly, he (Winnicott, 1963) invited social workers to:

> …think of casework as providing a human basket. Clients put all their eggs into one basket which is you (and your agency). They take a risk, and first they must test you to see if you may be able to prove sensitive and reliable or whether you have it in you to repeat the traumatic experiences of their past. (p. 227)

J. Applegate (✉)
School of Social Policy and Social Work Practice, University of Pennsylvania, Philadelphia, PA 19130, USA
e-mail: jjapplelg@verizon.net

E. Ruderman and C. Tosone (eds.), *Contemporary Clinical Practice: The Holding Environment Under Assault*, Essential Clinical Social Work Series,
DOI 10.1007/978-1-4614-4124-3_2,

Expanding the scope of the holding environment concept beyond caregiver–infant and clinician–client, Winnicott (1956) proposed an ecosystem model as well: "One can discern a series—the mother's body, the mother's arms, the parental relationship, the home, the family including cousins and near relations, the school, the locality with its police stations, the county with its laws" (p. 310). If he were alive today, he would likely broaden his conception further to include the national and global environments and the social policies that organize them. And, given the state of today's national and global environments, how might he characterize the integrity of the macro holding environment that we all inhabit now?

We submit that the following sociopolitical factors have deeply eroded the macro holding environment in ways that leave us and our patients subject to destabilizing chronic anxiety: the current crisis in health care (especially the commodification of care exemplified by managed care), the specter of terrorism, the chronic societal trauma of living in a nation engaged in distant brutal wars, the careless plundering of natural resources, the exploitative lending practices that have led countless families to bankruptcy, and the onslaught of media coverage designed to instill fear in our citizenry. We further suggest that these large-scale phenomena insidiously affect all the subsystems of the holding environment, including the settings in which we conduct clinical practice. Not only do we listen to and absorb clients' narratives of the stresses engendered by an eroded holding environment, we feel the effects of these stresses in our own daily lives, professional and personal.

Beyond its manifest effects, this backdrop of traumatic stress in our practice venues casts shadows of unease onto the unconscious transference/countertransference dialectic that shapes the core of psychoanalytically informed practice. The danger here is that, as we mobilize our own defenses to cope with a traumatogenic world, our reflective capacity to monitor our own inner lives is compromised in ways that impede optimal practice. Moreover, the vast scope of today's societal stress leaves us feeling stymied in knowing how best to initiate the reparative political and social activism that is so integral to social work's mission and legacy.

Winnicott (1970) asserted that, under conditions of a rupture in the continuity and felt safety of the holding environment, the developing baby experiences episodes of what he termed primitive agonies or unbearable anxieties—overwhelming feelings of being dropped, falling forever, or experiencing psychosomatic fragmentation. While most of our patients have moved developmentally beyond a vulnerability to such frightening regressions, echoes of these anxieties are likely aroused when they feel "dropped" by societal holding environments. The point here is that living in an environment that no longer "holds" them subjects our patients—and us—to a very basic form of survival anxiety that even the best ego defenses fail to temper.

The Holding Environment and Potential Space

According to the Winnicottian version of early development, as good-enough caregivers provide thousands of holding functions, babies develop an illusion that their needs at a given moment are magically met. Because attuned caregivers "read" the baby's needs as they arise, they foster in the baby an illusion of omnipotence—"when I need you,

I can make you appear!" Later, with increasing cognitive and emotional development, the baby begins to show signs of becoming more affect-tolerant and self-regulating, signaling caregivers that they do not need to be so perfectly attuned. Busy with something else, they may not rush so quickly in response to the baby's cry. In the increasingly frequent temporal "spaces" between the baby's need and the caregivers' responses, he or she begins to experience a sense of separation between self and others. The illusion of omnipotence gives way to experiences of disillusionment, setting the stage for self-object differentiation and further development.

To cope with their disillusionment, most babies find a caregiver substitute—a blanket, soft toy, or other transitional object that feels, smells, and comforts in ways that evoke the image of the primary caregiver (Winnicott, 1953). Witnessing this developmental milestone, we conclude that the baby has begun to internalize the holding functions of caregivers to be able to self-soothe. Interestingly, this phenomenon typically occurs at around 6 months, the age at which attachment theorists believe a working model of attachment is taking shape. Winnicott (1953) believed that the appropriation of a transitional object is the baby's first truly creative act. He or she has reached into the inanimate environment to find an object that is imbued with caregiving functions. Holding that object, he or she can conjure an image of the primary caregiver. The object acts as a symbolic bridge over the newly experienced space between self and others, person and environment.

Though the transitional object phenomenon is especially prevalent in the western caregiving contexts, babies universally evince some form of transitional process that enables them to tolerate the anxiety associated with separation-individuation (Applegate, 1989). Other transitional phenomena include lullabies, bedtime stories, prayers, and cultural rituals that become aspects of the baby's internalized holding environment. Again, they serve to bridge the space between me and not me, an intermediate area of experiencing that Winnicott termed "potential space"—the quietly alive, creative, interactional field wherein fantasy, dreaming, imagination, and play flourish. It is the enlivened area between objective reality and our subjectively constructed conceptions of reality. Winnicott (1953) believed that it is in this metaphorical "space" that we gain the capacity for play and an appreciation for art, music, and religious experiences.

Further, Winnicott (1971) proposed that this potential space is the location of cultural experience. In his formulation, cultural experience becomes an extension of "creative living first manifested in play" (p. 100). Elaborating this idea, Winnicott (1971) continues:

> I have used the term cultural experience as an extension of the idea of transitional phenomena and of play without being certain that I can define the word "culture". The accent indeed is on experience. In using the word culture I am thinking of the inherited tradition. I am thinking of something that is in the common pool of humanity, into which individuals and groups of people may contribute, and from which we all draw *if we have somewhere to put what we find.* (p. 99, italics in original)

The italicized proviso in Winnicott's last sentence is significant as we consider the current state of sociopolitical affairs. This cautionary note implies that there must be a lively collaborative potential space in which humanity can creatively provide conditions for a supportive holding environment and from which we can draw a sense of safety and enlivening sustenance.

The Collapse of Potential Space

We know that, as a result of trauma and/or chronic stress, the individual's capacity to sustain a reliable mental representation of a secure holding environment is compromised. In turn, both the transitional process and the potential space it generates lose flexibility. Winnicott's formulations about collective potential space suggest that this outcome can apply to the culture as a whole, leading ultimately to the collapse of potential space. We suggest that the collective anxiety associated with the separation panic of being "dropped" by society's "holding" institutions fosters regression to more and more primitive defenses, notably splitting and projection.

We witness evidence of collective splitting and projection on a daily basis. In the absence of potential space within which to encounter the complexity and novelty of human difference with respectful curiosity, our current leaders appear to resort defensively to a split "we–they" representation of the other. Projection serves the purpose of allowing the projectors to avoid awareness of owning thoughts, feelings, or desires that are experienced as ego-dystonic and anxiety arousing. This avoidance is accomplished by placing these internal phenomena outside the self and into groups of others who are targeted consciously as "different," but who are perceived, at an unconscious level, as similar. This process helps the projecting group establish a sense of distance between itself and its disowned parts. Anxiety is kept at bay by defining itself by contrast to the "others" who appear to carry the rejected elements (Lichtenberg, van Beusekom, & Gibbons, 1997).

Psychodynamic thinkers are accustomed to understanding phenomena such as racism, sexism, and homophobia in these terms. At the national/global level, we theorize that the preservation of "our" democratic ideals depends on the violent defeat of a vast "evil empire" of threatening others who appear to embody "our" disowned impulses. The "we–they" configuration generated by such xenophobia makes it possible to dehumanize others and fosters regression to a paranoid-schizoid position (Klein, 1946) that legitimizes oppression and, in the case of war and genocide, torture and elimination of them. Further, the resulting conflict between the two factions joins them in a kind of aversive fusion, closing the potential space for diplomacy and negotiation as adaptive means of problem solving. What is left is fertile ground in which splitting and projection can flourish.

Whither Solutions?

Overwhelmed by the scope of chronic societal stress and trauma, the tendency is toward a resigned passivity. Such a posture leaves the potential space for creative dialogue collapsed. As psychoanalytically informed social workers accustomed to thinking in more activist terms, we are left with a sense of impotence and guilt. One antidote to these feelings is a forceful return to the kind of social action that energized our social work ancestors and served us well during the 1960s and 1970s. There are lessons to be learned by revisiting the revolutionary potential of applied psychoanalysis. Herein lies the potential for reopening the collective potential space for creative problem solving.

Examples include work by Volkan (1988, 1997) who employs psychoanalytic theory in addressing interethnic and international conflict and violence. He underscores the dynamics of projection as a crucial element of the apparent need for many large sociopolitical groups to have enemies and allies. In applying his formulations to diplomacy, he emphasizes the need for analytically informed consultants to gather conflicted groups in neutral venues to help them mourn collectively past traumas that have spawned generations of violence. Similarly, the political psychologist Ross (1995, 2000, 2001) applies object relations theory to diplomatic interventions aimed at peacemaking in large-scale ethnic conflicts. In an article entitled "Good-Enough Isn't So Bad: Thinking About Success and Failure in Ethnic Conflict Management" (Ross, 2000), he specifically uses Winnicottian concepts to explore the dynamics of diplomatic negotiation. Both of these scholars can be said to be reopening the collapsed "potential space" for healing and resolution.

These are but two of many theorists who are turning to applied psychoanalysis in their efforts to understand and intervene in social struggle. We can learn much from this body of scholarship, and such study has the potential to inform and reinvigorate our efforts to restore eroded and supportive holding environments for our patients and ourselves. As social workers, we know that this restoration must begin both inside and, through vigorous social action, outside our clinical practices. Inside the office, we can promote and model strategies of self-care and social engagement. Outside, we can write editorials, lobby our legislators, resist practices and policies that dehumanize us and our patients, and raise consciousness among our colleagues by staging conferences like the one exemplified by the symposium that generated this book.

The election of US president Barack Obama in 2008 offers an opportunity to begin to rebuild the sociopolitical holding environment so deeply eroded during the previous 8 years. By reaching out to engage other nations whose differences have led to their becoming objects of dehumanizing projection, this new administration can open the potential space for diplomatic dialogue that recognizes and respects the shared humanity of the global community. At the national level, the hope that energized the Obama campaign appears to be finding expression in social policies designed to provide for more equitable distribution of goods and services across the full spectrum of our citizenry. Nevertheless, as demonstrated by the upsurge of resistance against the 2009 efforts to realize the goal of universal health care, the need for our activism is as urgent as ever. Analytically informed social workers have unique perspectives and decades of experience to bring to the inevitable struggle that will accompany the process of social change.

References

Applegate, J. S. (1989). The transitional object reconsidered: Some sociocultural variations and their implications. *Child and Adolescent Social Work Journal, 6*, 38–51.

Applegate, J. S. (1997). The holding environment: An organizing metaphor for social work theory and practice. *Smith College Studies in Social Work, 68*, 7–29.

Klein, M. (1946). Notes on some schizoid mechanisms. *International Journal of Psycho-Analysis, 27*, 99–110.
Lichtenberg, P., van Beusekom, J., & Gibbons, D. (1997). *Encountering bigotry: Befriending projecting persons in everyday life*. Northvale, NJ: Jason Aronson.
Ross, M. H. (1995). Psychocultural interpretation theory and peacemaking in ethnic conflicts. *Political Psychology, 16*, 523–544.
Ross, M. H. (2000). "Good-enough" isn't so bad: Thinking about success and failure in ethnic conflict management. *Peace and Conflict: Journal of Peace Psychology, 6*, 27–47.
Ross, M. H. (2001). Psychocultural interpretations and dramas: Identify dynamics in ethnic conflict. *Political Psychology, 22*, 157–178.
Volkan, V. (1988). *The need to have enemies and allies: From clinical practice to international relationships*. Northvale, NJ: Jason Aronson.
Volkan, V. (1997). *Bloodlines: From ethnic price to ethnic terrorism*. New York, NY: Farrar, Straus & Giroux.
Winnicott, D. W. (1953). Transitional objects and transitional phenomena: A study of the first not-me possession. *International Journal of Psycho-Analysis, 34*, 89–97.
Winnicott, D. W. (1956). The antisocial tendency. In *Through paediatrics to psychoanalysis* (pp. 306–315). New York, NY: Basic Books, 1975.
Winnicott, D. W. (1961). Varieties of psychotherapy. In *Home is where we start from* (pp. 101–111, Reprint in 1986). New York, NY: Norton.
Winnicott, D. W. (1963). The mentally ill in your caseload. In *The maturational processes and the facilitating environment* (pp. 217–229, Reprint in 1965). Madison, CT: International Universities Press.
Winnicott, D. W. (1970). The mother-infant experience of mutuality. In E. J. Anthony & T. Benedek (Eds.), *Parenthood: Its psychology and psychopathology* (pp. 245–256). Boston, MA: Little, Brown.
Winnicott, D. W. (1971). The location of cultural experience. In *Playing and reality* (pp. 95–103). London, England: Tavistock.

Chapter 3
Grief and Loss in an Age of Global Trauma: Protest and Despair Versus Attachment and Reorganization

Judith Kay Nelson

In a *New Yorker* article, James Wood analyzed the traumatic events reported in The *New York Times* on a single day, Thursday, May 15, 2008:

> The lead article was about the earthquake in China, now estimated to have killed more than fifty thousand people. It was titled "Tiny Bodies in a Morgue, and Unspeakable Grief in China," and was accompanied by a photograph of two parents sitting next to their dead child. A story about the recent cyclone in Myanmar estimated the number of deaths at anywhere between 28,833 and 127,990.... And the minor stories, on this day? At least ten people killed in a bomb attack west of Baghdad, in Abu Ghraib; a policeman killed in a bomb attack in northern Spain (probably ETA terrorists); a possible missile strike on a Pakistani border village that killed about a dozen people (this may well have been the work of an American drone); and a piece about a radical Islamic cleric, resident in Italy but "transferred," perhaps thanks to American help, by the process of "extraordinary rendition," to a jail in Egypt where he was allegedly tortured. (p. 116)

Looking at any day's newspaper or watching the television news would yield similar results. There is trauma of all kinds—war, violent crime, oppression, political repression, natural disasters—both down the street and around the world, and with today's media coverage and global accessibility, increasingly there is little difference between the two locations. Global trauma is a term used to refer to these events that daily impact individuals and groups around the world, whether directly through personal experience or indirectly for those who experience trauma vicariously through witnessing or media exposure (Kaplan, 2008; Narine, 2010).

Global PTSD is a term describing the effects of global trauma on individuals (Begec, 2007; Wiley-Blackwell, 2010). It is discussed, for example, in the NATO "Security Through Science" series (Begec, 2007) that describes research, diagnosis, and treatment of combat veterans from countries around the globe—Croatia, Canada, Georgia, Vietnam, Iraq, Afghanistan, and the USA—and survivors of

J.K. Nelson (✉)
The Sanville Institute for Clinical Social Work and Psychotherapy,
Berkeley, CA 94710, USA
e-mail: jkaynelson@sbcglobal.net

E. Ruderman and C. Tosone (eds.), *Contemporary Clinical Practice: The Holding Environment Under Assault*, Essential Clinical Social Work Series,
DOI 10.1007/978-1-4614-4124-3_3, © Springer Science+Business Media New York 2013

terrorism at the World Trade Center and in the Middle East. A collective view of PTSD affecting whole groups of people following a collective trauma is a possibility that has not been considered in the literature so far, though it seems worth considering in situations when natural disasters or wars touch the lives of an entire population. Collective PTSD seems visible and palpable in countries like Haiti following the earthquake in Port-au-Prince in 2010 or in New Orleans in 2005 after the Hurricane Katrina or after the 2004 Indonesian tsunami, not to mention countries completely torn apart by war.

Global grief, sometimes referred to as "vicarious bereavement" (Rando, 2010), is a term that has been used to describe everything from the worldwide response to high-profile losses such as 9/11 (British Broadcasting Corporation, 2001) and the death of singer Michael Jackson (Associated Press, 2009), to people threatened by climate change, oil prices, or the real estate and banking crises. The idea behind global grief is that the impact of the loss is so widespread that it touches off grief reactions in a great many individuals. Most authors reserve the term global grief for those directly impacted by these losses. However, Chochinov (2005) points out that one need not directly experience the trauma in order to feel its effects.

Vicarious grief is defined as grief experienced on behalf of another person through "imaginative or sympathetic participation" (Rando, 2010, p. 1) in the experience of another person's loss. While this term has primarily been applied to people who know, work with, or are related to the victim or the bereaved, vicarious grief may also occur in the absence of a personal relationship when people suffer over someone else's loss as if it were their own. Certain qualities of the event, including "suddenness, violence, preventability, and child loss" (Rando, 2010, p. 1), are particularly gripping to a great many people. Continual exposure to media reports of human suffering, loss, and trauma overexposes people to graphic images creating "vicarious trauma" (Kaplan, 2008) leading to vicarious grief. Referring to the 2011 earthquake, tsunami, and nuclear reactor crises in Japan, Hunsberger (2011) writes, "We can view these horrifying events…within minutes of their happening. Thanks to YouTube and smartphones, we can watch a tsunami devastate a town as if it were happening across the street and check a nuclear reactor's status on Twitter" (D1). Human-inflicted trauma causes the most intense grief reactions for individuals and presumably therefore also for groups. Examples would be the September 11, 2001, attacks on the World Trade Center, the Oklahoma City bombing, the Columbine school massacre, as well as the violent deaths of famous individuals such as Princess Diana or President John Kennedy. As poet Robert Burns (1784/2010) wrote, "Man's inhumanity to man/Makes countless thousands mourn!"

Rando (2010) identifies two types of vicarious grief. The first occurs when a person identifies with the experiences of a victim, putting himself or herself in the same psychological position. The second type is more severe and impacts the functioning of the vicarious mourner who is left feeling "stunned and overwhelmed" (p. 2). Rando suggests that this can occur when "the individual's assumptive world is rendered invalid by the death…" threatening the "mental set, derived from past personal experience, that contains all a person assumes, expects, and believes to be true about the self, the world and everything and everyone it" (p. 2).

The trauma, disaster, and death and dying literatures, along with the media, diagnose global trauma, global PTSD, and global grief and suggest cutting-edge treatment protocols. Primarily, however, they focus on these phenomena at a one-person level, meaning that the tragic wave of global traumatization and its effects must be healed one person at a time. Global diagnosis and treatment for these particular forms of global suffering are left to humanitarian and spiritual leaders.

Attachment theory and research, however, offer a means for bridging the personal and the communal by giving us a way to make sense of what is happening in the global village, why it is happening, and possible remedies for mental health practitioners to consider as members of our own social and cultural groups as well as in work with clients and patients. An attachment approach highlights the importance of the common human bonds that are forged through loss, trauma, and oppression and our grief reactions to these extreme, ongoing losses. Our shared human attachment and caregiving systems cross cultural boundaries and offer a vehicle for understanding ourselves, a means of transforming our grief and loss into new attachments, and a guide to healing and hope.

Attachment, Loss, and Grief

Attachment—the way in which we form intimate bonds—and the reactions that occur the process that occurs when those bonds are threatened, interrupted, or severed, are at the heart of attachment theory. Attachment is necessary for the survival of our infants—a necessity that carries forward into adulthood in preparation for parenting and also as a means of maintaining security and regulating distress. Grief is the built-in biological response that occurs following separation from attachment figures (Nelson, 2005). Painful reactions to separations from attachment figures are ubiquitous, and powerful and work as a powerful incentive to protect and preserve the attachment bond.

British psychoanalyst John Bowlby (1969), the father of attachment theory, noticed that the juvenile offenders with whom he worked had numerous traumatic separations in their early backgrounds. Then, during WWII when British infants and children were sent to nurseries out of harm's way from the bombings, he had the opportunity to view the impact of traumatic separations on infants first hand (Bowlby, 1960). What he noticed was that they went through a predictable sequence of grief reactions: protest, despair, and finally—if there was no reunion with the parental caregiver and no acceptable substitute—detachment and even death.

Bowlby (1960) pointed out that upon separation the infants would first cry loudly, shake their cribs, and in general protest with vocal urgency and much physical activity. These protest behaviors had one aim: to signal the parent to come back. Reunion was the only acceptable outcome. If, after a period of protest, there was no reunion, Bowlby (1960) noted, the infants would enter a state of despair in which they would wail quietly but intermittently and slump in the corner of their cribs, in the universally recognized posture of hopelessness and despair. The state of active protest would give way to this quiet despair, as they appeared to give up all hope for reunion—hence the quiet wail interspersed with silence.

If these infants left in institutions away from their parents did not experience a reunion after a prolonged period of despair and the child was unable to connect with a consistently available substitute, the child would then descend into a life-threatening state of silent detachment (Bowlby, 1960). I have noted this state of detachment even in still photographs of children separated and traumatized by the loss of their parents in wars and natural disasters. Their eyes are glazed over and they appear unable to find any spark of life or to establish relationships with potential helpers who are unfamiliar to them. If the loss is permanent and no relatives or permanent nurturing caregivers are found, these children may die, even though their physical needs are attended to by aid workers (Bowlby, 1960; Nelson, 2005; Spitz, 1946).

Bowlby (1961) noted parallels between the processes of mourning after separations in infancy and those of adults grieving at the death of a close loved one. "[W]hen he weeps the bereaved adult is responding to loss as a child does to the temporary absence of his mother" (p. 333). Adults, too, experience protest and despair. The difference is that adult grief can be resolved or transformed through what Bowlby termed "reorganization" rather than necessarily ending in the potentially fatal detachment of infancy—though that too has its parallel in adult grief reactions that stall in detached depression.

In my work applying an attachment perspective to adult crying (Nelson, 2005), I came to see that protest, despair, and detachment are phases of grief that apply not just to separation and loss of close attachment figures but to grief reactions in response to all kinds of losses—major and minor, literal and symbolic, real and imagined, and personal and vicarious. Each stage of grief sends different emotional messages to potential caregivers and provokes different kinds of responses in them, or, as we say clinically, different kinds of countertransference reactions.

Protest

Protest in adulthood, as in infancy, is aimed at undoing or avoiding a loss and bringing about a reunion, recovery, or reconciliation. All the grief energy goes into reestablishing the threatened connection and fighting any indication that the loss is irrevocable or permanent. The internal state that accompanies it ranges from anger and rage to hurt feelings, frustration, denial, and disbelief. Protest, even when accompanied by tears, has a hostile, demanding, and sometimes accusatory edge that results in alienating potential caregivers who may feel not empathic but distanced, irritated, or apathetic. The protest grief of others can feel blaming, critical, and guilt inducing—and this is no less true of the protest grief of groups. Even when sympathy is felt and offered, those protesting their losses are not usually responsive: they want action, not comfort (Nelson, 2005).

Protest does serve an evolutionary attachment purpose: it is designed to be an effective emergency signal to bring about reunion after a traumatic and potentially life-threatening separation (Bowlby, 1969). On a personal level and at the communal level, we see protest functioning to avert losses, to undo threats, and to resolve conflicts. In some instances, this can be a viable, healthy, and productive way to mobilize and avoid further traumatization.

In the 1980s when HIV/AIDS activism was just beginning, my oldest daughter joined forces with Aids Coalition to Unleash Power (ACT UP), an in-your-face political action group that took on drug companies, insurance companies, the medical establishment, and government bureaucracies (ACT UP.org, 2011). Their motto was "Silence = Death." Because they did not want to face death or see others do so, they protested in highly visible ways, frequently getting arrested and fined. In the end, they succeeded not only in increasing awareness about HIV but also in bringing about much needed social change and the release of experimental drugs that transformed HIV into a chronic illness rather than a terminal one for many (Medley, 1996).

The problem comes when a person—or a group—is permanently protesting ongoing losses, or losses so overwhelming that surrender or acceptance are not felt to be possible. Despair is avoided at all costs by prolonging the protest. From a psychoanalytic viewpoint, we see that continual protest—an aggressive demand for restoration of the lost object—can be a way of symbolically and defensively maintaining a connection to that lost object (Freud, 1917/1989).

Protest also becomes problematic on a communal level when group protest against real, imagined, or threatened losses is socially sanctioned and expressed in aggressive language, armed aggression, terrorism, torture, threats, blame, criticism, and demands—violent "protests" of all kinds. As with individuals, social groups who remain stuck in the protest stage of grief cannot work it through to the stage of reorganization. Attachments cannot be reconfigured, and reconciliations cannot be achieved. Victory or conquest becomes the only end: what has been lost must be restored at any cost. Potential caregivers and allies are casualties of this process as they are by definition part of the problem rather than part of the solution, thereby reinforcing intergroup tensions and cutting off possible avenues for reorganization, resolution, or repair (Mikulincer & Shaver, 2007; Nelson, 2005, 2010).

Despair

Despair, like protest, has both a healthy and a pathological manifestation. Despair corresponds to the abject, helpless, and hopeless acceptance of the fact of a loss—which is sometimes called surrender. On the one hand, surrender is necessary in working through grief. Unlike the often alienating forces of protest, despair can trigger a strong sympathetic pull toward the sufferer—from close caregivers to strangers. By acknowledging the painful permanence of the loss and reestablishing a symbolic connection with the lost attachment figure, there is energy available for connecting with new attachment figures or for reconfiguring the relationships with surviving ones—Bowlby's (1961) definition of reorganization. Because receiving care is intrinsic to maintenance of the attachment bond, it must also be part of the healing process for despairing adults—either through internalized objects or through direct aid and comfort from others.

Despair can be seen as a necessary stage in moving through and transforming grief. It can however also result in immobilizing sadness characterized by helplessness and hopelessness. As clinicians, we understand and work with this despair in individuals. As social workers, we also understand that seemingly insurmountable losses can immobilize despairing social groups who seem stunned or numbed by loss to the point where their energies are drained, creativity sidelined, and hope overwhelmed. Cumulative or repetitive trauma resulting in learned helplessness may also contribute to chronic despair in social groups (Simkin, Lederer, & Seligman, 1983). Social groups, too, may become unreachable in their detached depression when they are too withdrawn to accept overtures from potential caregivers (Everett, 2010; Mikulincer & Shaver, 2007).

Reorganization

Bowlby (1980) described reorganization—the resolution of grief from an attachment viewpoint—as the bereaved coming gradually to accept that "the loss is indeed permanent and that life must be shaped anew" (p. 93). It is necessary then, Bowlby wrote, to discard former ways of being, thinking, and behaving in order to develop new patterns and ways of being, which makes despair and depression almost inevitable during the grief process. Under optimal circumstances, despair may gradually begin to alternate with a slightly more hopeful assessment of the new situation and new ideas about how to adapt it. This process includes "reshaping internal representational models so as to align them with the changes that have occurred in the bereaved's life situation" (Bowlby, 1980, p. 94). With reorganization, one must "fill unaccustomed roles" and "acquire new skills," which comes about, not through a "mere release of affect," Bowlby notes, but rather through "a cognitive act on which all else turns" (p. 94).

After years on the battle lines with ACT UP, my daughter, for example, left behind the takeovers and picket lines and went to nursing school, becoming a nurse practitioner specializing in HIV/AIDS and currently working as part of the UC San Francisco team that handles treatment for HIV-positive prisoners throughout California. Mothers Against Drunk Driving reorganize their grief into another kind of action. Valentino Achak Deng, one of the "Lost Boys of the Sudan," who survived unbearable trauma, grief, and dislocation and loss, collaborated on telling his life story in the novel *What Is the What* (Eggers, 2006). His unbearable pain was thereby transformed into a work of fiction that helps to educate Westerners about the Sudanese Civil War, provides funds to help his surviving family and community, and supports political and social efforts aimed at helping other traumatized dislocated Sudanese young people like himself.

While I have been working on this chapter, I have been looking for examples of people who are involved in helping all of us transform our global grief into global reorganization. There are great numbers of visionary individuals and groups—politicians, religious, spiritual, and business leaders—working to inspire us to rethink and retool our notions about global interconnectedness. There are nonprofits, schools, and health and social welfare organizations helping to guide us in the direction of redefining and reorganizing our attachments and caregiving relationships to each other on a global scale.

The Greater Good Science Center (2009) at the University of California, Berkeley, defines global compassion as concern for and commitment to people beyond one's immediate family or community. At globalcompassion.com (2009), an organization devoted to worldwide consciousness raising on behalf of people living with HIV/AIDS, they point out that "compassion starts with seeing others and learning their stories." Henry Wadsworth Longfellow (1866) put it similarly when he said, "If we could read the secret history of our enemies, we should find in each man's life, sorrow and suffering enough to disarm all hostility." The same media that passes along the news of traumatic events also passes along the stories of individuals and communities, the pictures, and the films that invite compassion rather than judgment and caring and love rather than hatred and revenge. Clinicians also play a role in global reorganization by addressing individual trauma through the therapeutic attachment bond. Helping to increase attachment security is a giant first step toward global empathy and global caregiving. Attachment researchers Mikulincer and Shaver (2007) write that attachment security, created by "interactions with available and supportive attachment figures"—parents, partners, therapists—maximizes the chances that an individual will be able to "create positive beliefs about other people," their "sensitivity, responsiveness, and goodwill" (p. 38).

Securely attached individuals also rely less on defenses that distort their perceptions of interpersonal and intergroup interactions and increase the risk of conflict. Mikulincer and Shaver, studying secular Israeli Jewish students, found that "the higher a participant's attachment anxiety, the more negative and hostile his or her appraisals of Israeli Arabs, ultra-Orthodox Jews, Russian immigrants, and homosexuals" (p. 185). The anxiously attached students were also more likely to consider these other groups as threatening. Research has also shown that attachment insecurity "interferes with compassion toward suffering strangers, members of minority groups, and members of the community with special needs" (Mikulincer & Shaver, 2007, p. 341). Insecurely attached individuals express more severe judgments and punishments of moral transgressors and surprisingly, increased willingness to die for a cause. Insecure people, Mikulincer and Shaver write, "cling to particular cultural worldviews and derogate alternative views in an attempt to enhance their impoverished self-concepts and achieve a stronger sense of value and meaning" (p. 211).

Securely attached people, on the other hand, feel that being part of a loving, connected human can be:

> a pathway to self-transcendence.... It promotes a sense of symbolic immortality, making it less necessary to validate one's worldview and promote oneself and one's own group. This suggests...that fostering attachment security might contribute to world peace, whereas making people feel insecure, either dispositionally (in families) or contextually (in political speeches), may contribute to perpetual conflict and premature death. (Mikulincer & Shaver, 2007, p. 210)

In five different studies of the secular Israeli Jewish students mentioned earlier, Mikulincer and Shaver (2007) found that momentarily activating mental representations of attachment figure availability (either by subliminally presenting security-related words, such as "love" and "closeness," or by asking participants to read a story or visualize the face of a supportive relationship partner) eliminated negative responses to a variety of outsider groups. That is to say that merely being asked to create mental representations of available attachment figures promoted more tolerant and accepting attitudes toward people who did not belong to the study participants' own social group. "[E]mpathy, compassion and generous altruistic responses to needy others" (pp. 69–70) also increased, even in those with anxious attachment styles.

Caregiving, the behavioral system that complements and mirrors the attachment system, though primarily evolved to increase the viability of one's own offspring and close relatives, may also have been more generally adapted to respond to the needs of extended families and tribal societies. Individuals who have experienced positive, nurturing, and affect-regulating caregiving experiences early in life are also more able to feel compassion, empathy, and generosity toward people outside their own immediate nuclear family who may be suffering or in need (Mikulincer & Shaver, 2007).

Even formal education—both secular and religious—can influence the values that impact the caregiving system into concern for the extended human community. This may be accomplished by stressing concepts such as the global village and the human family and extending the concept of respecting elders and designating "brothers and sisters" as a term for other people in the larger world. In this way, the caregiving system is activated whenever attachment needs, wounds, or pain is encountered in any human beings around the world.

Art is another means for powerfully transforming (or as we would say here, reorganizing) people's hearts and minds. In his book on Afghan culture, Dyck (2008) writes about an Uzbek poet Alisher Nava'i who challenged people of his time—the fourteenth and fifteenth centuries in northern Afghanistan—to greater human compassion. One of his poems, "The Conference of the Birds," which is awkwardly translated into English from early Uzbek language, points out that while there is much suffering in life, the best way to move through it is by reaching out to the suffering of others:

> The world built via hardship is a sorrow's place,
> Here all people meet with sorrow face to face.
> Global grief is in the heart of all nations,
> It grows more with each passing generation.
> However, those who close to people remain,
> [Are more able to] weather their road's pain.
> Whoever from their [own] pain needs to find relief,
> [Would do well to] lessen [an]other's grief. (pp. 1–2)

Our trauma is global, our grief is global, and our reorganization must be global as well.

References

ACT UP New York. (2011). http://www.actupny.org

Associated Press. (2009, June 26). Global grief over death of Michael Jackson. NEWSONE for Black America. http://newsone.com/entertainment/associated-press/global-grief-over-death-of-michael-jackson/

Begec, S. (Ed.). (2007). *The integration and management of traumatized people after terrorist attacks* (Vol. 15). Amsterdam, The Netherlands: IOS.
Bowlby, J. (1960). Grief and mourning in early childhood. *Psychoanalytic Study of the Child, XV*, 9–52.
Bowlby, J. (1961). Process of mourning. *The International Journal of Psycho-analysis, 45*(4–5), 317–339.
Bowlby, J. (1969). *Attachment* (Vol. I). New York, NY: Basic Books.
Bowlby, J. (1980). *Loss: Sadness and depression* (Vol. III). New York, NY: Basic Books.
British Broadcasting Corporation. (2001). Grappling with global grief. BBC News, 1. http://news.bbc.co.uk/2/hi/uk_news/1539794.stm
Burns, R. (1784/2010). Man was made to mourn. classiclit.about.com/library/bl-etext/rburns/bl-rburns-manmade.htm
Chochinov, H. M. (2005). Vicarious grief and response to global trauma. *The Lancet, 366*(9487), 697–698.
Dyck, G. (2008). The Timurid renaissance of Northern Afghanistan and the poet Alisher Nava'i's inspiring humanitarian model. *Navoi's Garden*, 1–3. http://www.navoigarden.com/articles.htm
Eggers, D. (2006). *What is the what: The autobiography of Valentino Achak Deng*. San Francisco, CA: McSweeney's.
Everett, J. E. (2010). Policy implication of attachment processes in adulthood: Caregiving and family preservation. In S. Bennett & J. K. Nelson (Eds.), *Adult attachment in clinical social work: Practice, research and policy* (pp. 195–216). New York, NY: Springer.
Freud, S. (1917/1989). Mourning and melancholia. In P. Gay (Ed.), *The freud reader* (pp. 584–589). New York, NY: W.W. Norton.
Greater Good Science Center. (2009). Mission statement. greatergood.berkeley.edu/sci-about_landing.html
Global Compassion. (2009). www.globalcompassion.com. Accessed 7 Jan 2009.
Hunsberger, B. (2011). Keep global disasters in perspective. *The Sunday Oregonian*. D1, D3. Accessed 19 Mar 2011.
Kaplan, E. A. (2008). Global trauma and public feelings: Viewing images of catastrophe. *Consumption Markets and Culture, 11*(1), 3–24.
Longfellow, H. W. (1866). Driftwood: Tabletalk. In *Prose works of Henry Wadsworth longfellow* (Vol. III). Boston, MA: Ticknor & Fields.
Medley, R. (1996). ACT UP & TAG: A brief history of AIDS treatment ACTAGanism. *ACT UP*. www.actupny.org/treatment/Medley.html
Mikulincer, M., & Shaver, P. (2007). *Attachment in adulthood: Structure, dynamics and change*. New York, NY: The Guilford.
Narine, N. (2010). Global trauma and narrative cinema. *Theory, Culture & Society, 27*(4), 119–145.
Nelson, J. K. (2005). *Seeing through tears: Crying and attachment*. New York, NY: Routledge.
Nelson, J. K. (2010). Separation, loss, and grief in adults: An attachment perspective. In S. Bennett & J. K. Nelson (Eds.), *Adult attachment in clinical social work: Practice, research and policy* (pp. 79–95). New York, NY: Springer.
Rando, T.A. (2010). Vicarious bereavement. *Encyclopedia of death and dying, A-Bi*. http://www.deathreference.com/A-Bi/Bereavement-Vicarious.html.
Simkin, D. K., Lederer, J. P., & Seligman, M. E. P. (1983). Learned helplessness in groups. *Behaviour research and Therapy, 21*(6), 613–122.
Spitz, R. A. (1946). Anaclitic depression. *Psychoanalytic Study of the Child, 2*, 313–342.
Wiley-Blackwell. (2010). Leading practitioners recommend global PTSD treatment guidelines. *Science Daily*. http://www.sciencedaily.com/releases/2010/09/100928188711.htm.

Chapter 4
Integrating the Internal and External Worlds of Clinical Social Work: A Philosophical and Political Search

Rosalyn Benitez-Bloch

This chapter is a review of concepts from philosophy and psychoanalysis in their application to both clinical social work and our tradition of change agent. Having strayed from earlier values and traditions by stressing our clinical identification with other professions using psychoanalytic theory, we have lost our professional compass to the split. We need to reexamine our historical values and reintegrate them into more relevant responses to relieve the stresses of contemporary life. To recapture what we still prize of those lost values requires a conscious integration of our lives as citizens with our clinical work as they interact within the social environment that Winnicott called "transitional space" (Grolnick, Barkin, & Muensterberger, 1978). This is a complex process that many of us in the profession want to bridge.

To address what we have lost from our more unified professional past, we recall the philosophy inherent in the National Association of Social Workers (NASW) Code of Ethics (2008) that spells out our identity as both change agents and caseworkers, clinical and generic. Social changes after WWII, the growing impersonal corporate world of business and government, along with revolutionary technological advances are some of the major influences that have led to our feeling the loss of an earlier way of life.

The Individual and Loss

W.H. Auden (1940/1968) in his poem "The Unknown Citizen" describes this state of loss—a withering isolation; a concise brand-named generational history; a tribute to what was socially expected; a description of a compliant, passive citizen with no

---

Some ideas in this chapter came from discussions with Billie Lee Violette and Jane Rubin.

R. Benitez-Bloch (✉)
National Study Group, AAPCSW, USC and UCLA Schools of Social Work,
Los Angeles, CA 90049, USA
e-mail: rbloch6@roadrunner.com

E. Ruderman and C. Tosone (eds.), *Contemporary Clinical Practice: The Holding Environment Under Assault*, Essential Clinical Social Work Series,
DOI 10.1007/978-1-4614-4124-3_4, © Springer Science+Business Media New York 2013

known yearnings, no visible soul, who never expressed a desire for acknowledgement and, most important, did not complain.

> He was found by the Bureau of Statistics to be
> One against whom there was no official complaint,
> And all the reports on his conduct agree
> That, in the modern sense of the old-fashioned word, he was a saint,
> For in everything he did he served the Greater Community.
> Except for the War till the day he retired
> He worked in a factory and never got fired,
> But satisfied his employers, Fudge Motors Inc.
> Yet he wasn't a scab or odd in his views,
> For his Union reports that he paid his dues,
> (Our report on his Union shows it was sound)
> And our Social Psychology workers found
> That he was popular with his mates and liked a drink.
> The Press are convinced that he bought a paper every day
> And that his reaction to advertisements were normal in every way.
> Policies taken out in his name prove that he was fully insured,
> And his Health-card shows he was once in hospital but left cured.
> Both Producers Research and High-Grade Living declare
> He was fully sensible to the advantages of the Installment Plan
> And had everything necessary to the Modern Man.
> A phonograph, a radio, a car and frigidaire.
> Our researchers in Public Opinion are content
> That he held the proper opinions for the time of year;
> When there was peace, he was for peace; when there was war, he went.
> He was married and added five children to the population.
> Which our Eugenist says was the right number for a parent in his generation,
> And our teachers report that he never interfered with their education.
> Was he free? Was he happy? The question is absurd:
> Had anything been wrong, we should certainly have heard.

Complaints are the first step in moving toward social change as needs are recognized and acknowledged. Charles Taylor (1992) wrote, "Due recognition is not just a courtesy we owe people. It is a vital human need" (p. 26).

Our Historical and Cultural Context

Our profession is rooted in the concepts of the Enlightenment and the participation of the individual in a social environment. Locke, a leading philosopher of the Enlightenment, took earlier ideas about the nature of man as a social self and member of a community and transformed them into the concept of the social contract—namely, that when a man is born, he is already a member of a civil society, is at once part of a community in which there is a reciprocal relationship. Though born into an existing community, Locke proposed that the human mind, by divine design, was *tabula rasa* at birth, with the inherent capacity to develop it, to think, communicate, and engage with others in communal social life (Honderich, 1995).

Economics is one form of community social engagement. Adam Smith developed an economic theory about wealth, labor, and property, particularly around work, which he elucidated in *The Wealth of Nations*. Smith theorized that the social and moral objectives of work gave oneself and others pleasure because work was doing good, and in so doing, one helps self and the community. Through work, one also accumulates wealth, which he considered a sign of goodness (Honderich, 1995). Weber (1958), in *The Protestant Ethic and the Spirit of Capitalism,* further explored the thesis that Protestantism influenced the rise of modern capitalism by positing work as God's will and as such the highest form of moral behavior, which *ergo* made capitalism a moral system.

Weber (1958) emphasized the impact of the intersection of Calvinism with the end of feudal society and serfdom, a new time when a man could choose how and to whom to sell his labor, seemingly rendering work to be less harsh punishment and creating more of an independent economic relationship than slavery had been. Goodness became an effect of work, which also became a form of exchange through which to belong in society. Help for the needy from welfare systems was based on willingness to work as proof of moral acceptability. In the USA, help for the needy came to be conceptualized as unnecessary intervention in the flow of capitalism that would disturb the "natural self-regulation" of the market (a myth), as would institutions formed to benefit those who were in need. Not working was considered not only not "natural" but also as depriving people of motivation and of a road toward goodness and even spiritual salvation. To remove the threat of hunger and offer welfare without work meant, to those who were developing policy, removal of both the motive and the need to look for work; further, welfare would interfere with the pursuit of profits by owners and employers who needed laborers.

What were the social changes that brought about a need for public welfare agencies and community response to support those unemployed and needy? The industrial revolution both transplanted work from family enterprise to the larger cities, opened immigration, and loosened family, community, and religious bonds. Rural populations streamed into the cities. Some required economic help in this transition. Others were sent back from where they came if they were not needed to work or they were deemed of low moral character. The evidence of lack of moral character was need itself, tautological proof of their "unfitness" (Weber, 1958). Social Darwinism has always been misinterpreted as a philosophy supporting survival of the fittest (skipping over that "fit" may have developed from a mutation) and has been interpreted for convenience as well as misinterpreted and exploited for racist and eugenic purposes, most systematically by the Nazis (Honderich, 1995).

As neither religious communities nor private organizations could provide all that was needed, the public domain had to take responsibility for those who lived within the community. The economic–political policies of the time ran counter to the philosophy of natural human rights in which each member of society is entitled to be given certain assurances for survival. Social workers have often been caught between these two positions and have found themselves obligated in their jobs to carry out stringent and sometimes punitive policies.

Social Values and Fairness and Its Connection to Empathy

A modern philosophical basis of social fairness began to develop as a result of a more articulate working population, the rise of the union movement, and influences from immigrants who had come from societies who had already fought for human rights. The changing sociopolitical philosophy was reflected in the US Constitution (Barry, 1989).

John Rawls, a political philosopher of the 1970s and 1980s, defines justice as fairness in this way:

> All social primary goods—liberty and opportunity, income and wealth and the bases of self respect—are to be distributed equally unless an unequal distribution of any or all of these goods is to the advantage of the least favored. (Barry, 1989, p. 52)

Following the tradition of Locke, Rawls' theory of justice imagines people in a society entering into an abstract social contract, establishing fundamental principles for their life together, whatever happens in their future. He calls this part of the process "the original position"; it is an imagined situation in which people do not know what their future positions will be but maintain that all positions will be open and equal in opportunity (Barry, 1989).

Forcing us to choose and to not know what our own individual future position in the society might be ensures fairness. Rawls describes this imaginary state of setting aside our individual characteristics as "the veil of ignorance" about the future. We cannot know which particular person will be intellectually or physically gifted or impaired, healthy or chronically ill, single or married, rich or poor and what they might need as a result. This is hidden, but principles are founded on equality, respect, and values (Barry, 1989).

These key principles of the original position are agreed upon values for the self-respect of each member. Self-respect includes being just and fair to oneself and equally so to all other individuals. Being in a veil of ignorance, according to Rawls, we cannot imagine our future experiences or needs, but we must have these values securely in place so that we can respond fairly with compassion and empathy to individuals when the occasion arises (Barry, 1989).

The sense of justice is nurtured by society and needs to be maintained by its members. From my clinical perspective, it begins in the family. If parents understand that when children are loved, cared for, and treated fairly by parents, they internalize both a respectful sense of self and of others with a capacity to identify and empathize with others in school and in other social relationships. As children mature, they continue on course to develop and internalize justice and fairness both as a way of behaving in relationships and also as abstract principles, applicable not just to immediate associates but also to all people and to their own future.

Psychoanalysis has confirmed the validity of the process of this evolution through years of studying child development as it has been applied to family life, education, etc. These values cannot exist without social supports of individuals and families that provide a holding environment allowing them to blossom. Social work has often provided those supports; the inclusion of the methods of psychoanalysis has enriched social work practice, allowing individuals to access primitive feelings that deal with universal experiences, such as the sense of terror each of us experiences in feeling alone in the world. The ability to access primitive feelings enables the development of compassion for others as well as for oneself. Being with a therapist can help one feel less desolate in confronting and working through traumatic experiences of loneliness, adding a deeper dimension to the concept of relationship. Gaining awareness and dealing with such trauma in our own unique experiences leaves us open to the possibility of empathy with others. Psychoanalysis was empathic from its beginnings, both individually and socially (Danto, 2006).

I have found in my clinical practice that treating people with empathy and as equals does not always mean treating them the same; it means giving equal respect to an individual's capacities for self-realization. This also means acting affirmatively to remove inequalities that have disadvantaged some but do not invade another's fair share. In sports, it is called a "handicap" to compensate or redress those who have a disadvantage. Some of our civil rights legislation and our anti-age and gender discrimination laws are in this category of social justice.

Historical and Political Trends in Psychoanalysis

Unlike the political influences in the USA, the social democratic philosophy of Europe at the time of Freud already encompassed a strong social conscience. Psychoanalysts were vocal in their beliefs as well as in their sense of responsibility to provide services to all economic classes through free mental health centers. There were at least ten cities and seven countries in Middle Europe (Vienna, Budapest, etc.) with private clinics where psychoanalysts volunteered time. "[A]nalysts saw themselves as brokers of social change for whom psychoanalysis was a challenge to conventional political codes, a social mission more than a medical discipline" (Danto, 2006, p. 4). Perhaps having been in the midst of the human destruction of World War I propelled these analysts toward affirming life, moving away from aggression, and converting their beliefs into social action to attempt to preserve humanism.

In Central Europe, the climate was ripe for a more philosophical, less religious exploration of the inner life of man than in the USA, and that was what psychoanalysis was able to illuminate. At one time, philosophy and psychology were considered to be one subject. Freud was influenced by many philosophers such as Leibniz and Kant, who conceptualized that there was a mental space of which we were not aware which became the seed of the idea of the unconscious.[1] Brentano's ideas of inner awareness and experiencing mental phenomena as having intention also influenced him (Danto, 2006). Pappenheim believed that social change should reach "into the structure of family relationships, the social position of women and children

[1] Freud did not claim to discover the unconscious but to have assigned a place for the forces of conflict to exist.

[and] sexual reform" (Danto, 2006, p. 6). Freud was a product of this social democratic climate of Middle Europe. In 1921, he wrote "... and so from the very first individual psychology...is at the same time social psychology as well" (p. 4). The English analyst Bion (1922) echoed this theme when he wrote:

> The individual analyst has two main contacts: his patient and society.... It must therefore be borne in mind that the fundamental importance of our work demands the kind of fortitude and high morale which places the welfare of the analytic group and its work before the welfare of the individual analyst, and some times before the welfare even of a particular patient. This taken in conjunction with the isolation in which analyst and patient work, means that the analyst must possess a social consciousness of a very high degree.... Or, to put it another way, the analyst must never cease, even in the midst of his analytic work, to be a member of one or more social groups. (p. 24)

Diverse and revolutionary ideas flourished in Europe until the 1930s when fascism, the opposite of diversity and novelty, attempted to destroy social democracy, with its emphasis on conforming to an ideology that erased complexity, disavowed humanism, destroyed the achievements of the past, and tried to erase its memories, creating a vacuum leading to "cultural amnesia" (James, 2006).

By the time the Nazis and other fascist regimes came to power, many analysts, especially Jews including Freud, as well as politically outspoken non-Jews, had to leave their countries to survive. Some analysts were warned of impending danger by their patients during clinical hours. Others helped their analysts emigrate. At that time, politics was imminently present in the consulting room. To avoid it would have been suicidal as well as unreal. Many analysts immigrated to England where psychoanalysis was embraced and developed, over time, the Object Relations Theory, an internal relational perspective. Other analysts went to the USA where psychoanalysis was enfolded into the medical profession. Many lay analysts had difficulty attaining licenses to practice. In the USA, psychoanalysis evolved emphasizing ego psychology, a topographical and adaptive perspective that theoretically kept the analyst as the observer of the patient. This perspective had enormous influence on how countertransference was conceptualized and utilized (Conrad, 2007).

Leonard (1997) has credited the events of WWII for the breakdown in human values in the West, where mechanization and science were used to promote evil and war profiteering. The Nazis destroyed the European social contract when they rendered people stateless, without identity, propagating the myth that they were no longer members of any society, and therefore need not be considered human. The horror of the Holocaust may have contributed to emotional resistance and denial by many European analysts when they went to other countries where many retreated to a less involved political life, avoiding the pressures of social reality. For some, it was not easy to work with Holocaust survivors in a constant confrontation with trauma, and sometimes harder if the analyst were themselves also a survivor.

The afterlife of the political climate of Central Europe surrounding WWII has some parallels with our own time and the issues that therapists have to deal with both in and out of the consulting room. US participation in the Vietnam War was a trauma in which our souls were assaulted, and now we are dealing with US involvement in Iraq, Afghanistan, and Pakistan, the sites of injuries and deaths of young men and women. We are also responsible for treating those who survive both physically and psychologically.

Yet, the agonies and reality of the external world do not diminish the importance of the internal world. The outside is taken inside. In fact, Object Relations Theory, to which all psychoanalytically oriented professions ascribe, demonstrates that the taking in of the external world is the origin of perceptions of all primary object formation. As psychoanalysis in the USA developed, it also embraced Object Relations Theory, particularly the work of Melanie Klein, for whom the meaning of the external world became primarily a venue for the repetition and projections of earlier interior formed object relations unrelated to later social reality. It is ironic that Klein, a European analyst coming from a liberal society of social reform, chose to omit the social world, except by interpretation in object relations terms, relegating the social aspects of external life to that of symbolic deputies of the unconscious. It was equally ironic that US psychoanalysis focused on ego psychology and its concept of adaptation (Darwin's concept), despite being a culture born of revolution for social causes. The exception to this orientation in American psychiatry was Harry Stack Sullivan who, having grown up in poverty—an indisputable social reality—developed the environmental concept of interpersonal space (Danto, 2006).

The European analysts did not infuse American psychoanalysis with its social legacy, but most accepted the American medical model. For those who emigrated, perhaps that experience made sociopolitical activism feel less safe. There are still those analysts who have addressed social and political realities: Langer, Fromm, Simmel, Ferenzi, Horney, Alexander, Bettelheim, Fenichel, Deutsch, Reich, Jacobson, Piaget, Klein, Lacan, Bollas, Allderdice, Erikson, Balint, Samuels, Altman, and Kristeva. We might wonder why didn't they have more of an influence on American psychoanalysis?

American Social Work and Its Political Heritage

In the history of US social work, the works of Charlotte Towle, Helen Harris Perlman, Gordon Hamilton, Virginia Robinson, Lucille Austin, Bertha Reynolds, Jane Addams, and Mary Richmond formed the holistic and humanistic view of social work. One consistent theme was using the professional relationship to help people adapt and utilize the environment and another that the environment might also be influenced to adapt to individuals. These were the writers who proposed integrating social constraints with self-determination and empathy, a concept still presented in graduate education in social work.

In American social work, there has been a rich tradition of combining clinical work with social justice. Jane Addams stands as an icon because of her work at Hull House in Chicago where she combined housing opportunities and casework for poor people. Applegate (1997) states that she established what Winnicott would term a holding environment in the settlement house movement, as did the early Charity Organization Societies. Mary Richmond furthered this by developing the first clinical theory of casework as a result of her experiences in "friendly visiting." He further states "holding" has always been the relational backdrop of what social workers do in their various roles with individuals, families, groups, and communities, as well in psychotherapy (Applegate, 1997). In fact, Winnicott (cited in Applegate, 1997) stated "that casework might be described as the professionalized aspect of the normal function of parents and local units, a 'holding' of persons and of situations, while growth tendencies are given a chance" (p. 9). Applegate (1997) suggests that if Winnicott were alive today, "he would likely broaden his conception further to include national and global environments and the social policies that organize them."

It is my observation, as well as that of some colleagues, that before the 1960s, the social work profession was more unified, even as caseworkers were learning Freudian dynamics. There was a belief that social concerns and the individual were linked. That was a time of outstanding professional leadership and creative practice in social service agencies and in social policy. An example is Selma Fraiberg's (1959) successful experiment of applying psychodynamic theory in treating families in a public welfare agency to enable them to gain insight about their own behavior and make better choices. She demonstrated, as did Freud in his free clinics, that psychodynamic awareness need not be limited to the middle and upper classes but that poor people, even people on welfare, could also use this help to change. And this, in turn, could influence the social environment.

In the years that followed that creative period, it seems to me that we clinicians moved closer to the private practice model of psychology and psychoanalysis toward private money. We identified with the power model of the medical profession as if theirs was a more valuable approach (Conrad, 2007). Perhaps another influence on this professional splitting of the 1950s had to do with the McCarthy period, a time that made the fears and dangers of being a politically social person a reality in the USA in a way it had been previously. We were highly aware that the personal was political. We relinquished our identification with causes of social justice, which became, purportedly, the responsibility of nonclinical social workers, while the individual and family became the unit of our work. We have allowed influences from other professions to make intellectual knowledge and specialization more important than empathy, social justice, and fairness (Leonard, 1997). Did we relinquish part of our philosophical heritage for status?

The roots of American social work were connected to social institutions and political systems from its beginnings; there was awareness that economics played a role in the formation, impediments, and advantages of individual development and daily life. There was acknowledgement of the difference between neurotic suffering and common human deprivation. A professional ethic of responsibility prevailed, both as citizens and professionals, to attempt to implement changes that would move social institutions toward fairness. Yet, social work therapists in the USA were patronized by medical psychoanalysts as less clinical because they "diluted" themselves by espousing social causes. In contrast, European psychoanalysts' social concerns were never seen as abandoning or diluting its method or skills (Danto, 2006).

Sociopolitical factors have eroded the macro-holding environment (Applegate, 1997). Large-scale issues such as the health-care crisis in the USA, economic failure, and environmental depletion affect the subsystems of the holding environment including our own practice settings. These obvious phenomena

> cast shadows of unease onto the unconscious transference/countertransference dialectic that shapes the core of psychoanalytically informed practice. The danger here is that we mobilize our own defenses to cope with a traumatogenic world, and our reflective capacity to monitor our inner lives and associate to those of our patients is compromised. Given the scope of the problems we are at a loss as to best initiate reparative social activism so much a part of the social work mission and legacy. (Layton, Hollander, & Gutwill, 2006)

Our theme is neither new to social work nor outside of the psychoanalytic arena but is a reprise on a larger scale of earlier attempts to solve problems of justice and fairness as well as their effects on communities and individuals, some of whom are our patients.

The Present: Loss and the Stress of War

The pressures that stress us are many, but war is perhaps an overriding one that brings with it the loss of our young and the loss of our standing in the world. Jonathan Shay (1994, 2002), a psychiatrist at the V.A. in Los Angeles, has written two books using Homer's Iliad and the Odyssey, two epic classics that bring the issue of war into the consulting room. Each of the stories demonstrates the universality of personal wartime trauma and its aftermath through the characters of Achilles and Odysseus. In the Iliad, Achilles the beautiful and strong young man suffers unbearable rage and loss as well as narcissistic insult over what is taken from him. Odysseus has trouble, metaphorically, finding his way home from war, as do many of our veterans. Shay illustrates each book with cases from practice and describes how reading the epics can be of help to his patients who feel isolated from others and alien to humanity after having been soldiers at war. We are dealing with the same issues that Homer wrote of and the same issues that the analysts in Central Europe confronted but now on a far more complex and global scale.

Trauma and loss are inevitable, and mourning is a way toward hope and repair as we deal with despair. We are heirs to despair as the author Clive James (2006) wrote because "Ours was an age of extermination, an epoch of the abattoir" (p. xviii). We hope because there have been repairs to the world and still a sense of our being human continues to be present. "If the humanism that makes civilization civilized is to be preserved into this new century, it will need advocates. Those who advocate will need a memory, and part of that memory will need to be of an age in which they were not yet alive" (James, 2006, p. xviii). If one substitutes consciousness or awareness for alive, we are back in the clinical setting as well as with the not yetness of Rawls' veil of ignorance (Barry, 1989). Alive means being aware of one's history, conflicts, desires, fears, and wishes for the future. Often there is a veil of ignorance over both the origins of our personal history as well as our future development.

We are invaded by a rapid increase and volume of information (although it has its upside too) about war, political erosion, needs and traumas of all the world's people. In addition, there are assaults that are personal and as well as those we absorb from our patients. We feel overwhelmed, paralyzed, and then ineffective. Layton et al. (2006) call this the phenomenon of being in a "traumatogenic" environment. There is also more awareness of secondary trauma.

We ask the following: How separated are the internal and external worlds? How do they meet and where? How do political realities enter the transference and countertransference? What social traumas do we share? How does the outside world threaten the holding environment and containment of anxiety? What is the role of political ideology in fantasy life? Nazi ideology provided a social structure for Hitler and his followers to behave in reality based on shared unconscious fantasies projected onto and acted out in the external world. What are the basic human values of caring, feeling, and community? How can we provide ways to respond to them today? To not allow such questions about our social environment would seem to be to impose a dishonest superego censorship on our clinical practice.

Layton et al. (2006) state that now political themes appear increasingly in patient material (or not!). They discuss the need for psychotherapists to consider patients' concerns with events in the public realm as "real rather than as simply displacements or symbolic references to unconscious conflicts rooted in family and personal relationships" (p. 7). This is not a new theme for social work.

Miller-Florshein (2002), an Israeli analyst, writes about the common experience of patient and analyst in a country where shared violence is constant. She states:

> [Lifton (1978) and Lindy (1989)] believe that without an awareness of countertransference and its power, it is impossible to engage in meaningful therapy with survivors and comprehend their unexpressed pain; nor is it possible to arrive at a meaningful understanding of the unique forms of evil in our times. Therapists must be willing to reconsider social and scientific values they have believed in. For us, this means confronting our fears and hopes about our own death and survival, including our professional survival. The question arises as to whether, in our tumultuous reality, deprived of objective distance, we will have the ability to observe a process? Should we be speaking not about trauma victims and their therapists, but about *all of us* living in the shadow of trauma? Or is it perhaps precisely because of this, that we avoid discussing the difficult questions and dilemmas the situation imposes upon us. (pp. 73–74)

Or as Kristeva (1997) puts it:

> By recognizing our *uncanny* strangeness we shall neither suffer from it nor enjoy it from the outside. The foreigner is within me, hence we are all foreigners. Therefore Freud did not talk about them. The ethics of psychoanalysis implies a politics: it would involve a cosmopolitanism of a new sort that, cutting across governments, economics, and markets might work for a mankind whose solidarity is founded on the consciousness of its unconscious – desiring, destructive, fearful, empty, impossible….the ultimate condition of our being *with* others. (p. 284)

The opposite of this is the oversimplified idea of polarizing differences, creating an evil empire, the we–them configuration generated by our own disavowed impulses that foster and exploit regression to a paranoid–schizoid position for legitimizing war and closing the potential space for diplomacy. Our young soldiers then become sacrificial offerings in the name of power.

At the Los Angeles Institute and Society for Psychoanalytic Studies 2008 conference "The Soldier's Project," it was satisfying to experience the inclusion of the military (another culture), the vets, wives and parents of vets, the VA, etc. meeting together. The attendees, although coming from different perspectives, some of us professionals, were thus made to become aware of the others, difficult as it was, to accept some attitudes and challenged to give up our own particular position. There was an infusion of new meaning to community. It gave those of us who attended a feeling of renewal and hope that by forming a broader community, we had also found a different approach to dealing with the effects of war and the internal world.

These ideas represent a more personal involvement than what has usually been written about psychoanalysis and politics. Analysts such as Rangel, Moses, Lacan, Allderdice, Ross, Volkan, and Samuels have all focused intellectually on how psychoanalysis can frame social issues for deeper understanding of how psychoanalytic techniques can broker group differences. Both perspectives are nonjudgmental and objective but not experience-near, to use a term of Kohut, and they avoid the involvement of the emotional self.

Samuels (1993) writes:

> The political tasks of modern democracy are similar to the psychologists' tasks of modern therapy and analysis. In both areas there is a fight between consciousness, liberation and alterity on the one hand and suppression, repression, and omnipotent beliefs in final truths on the other. Both psychological and political processes share an uncertain outcome and live in the continuous process of change. (p. 4)

Both democracy and psychoanalysis are open systems and have infinite possibilities of interpretation.

Summary

The current question for all of us is: How can we try to make our inner world relatively harmonious with the comfort of one's good objects while also live as citizens? We cannot remain unconcerned about injustice and violence, but the pain and rage they engender leads to a resurrection of splitting and projections of the bad parts of ourselves. With a new national administration following the 2008 election of US President Barack Obama, we already have a better holding environment and opportunity for new policy.

Our task is to work to rebuild the eroded holding environment for ourselves and for our patients. This involves returning to former values while injecting them into new configurations in our professional lives. In treatment, we try to create, for both the clinician and the patient, a space and a process to help us live and struggle with the paradox of being an individual and also a member of society. We want our work with patients to inform us so that we can feed into our professional affiliations to link our knowledge base and our clinical experience with social policy as steps toward dissolving the paradox between inner and outer worlds.

References

Applegate, J. S. (1997). The holding environment: An organizing metaphor for social work theory and practice. *Smith College Studies in Social Work, 68*, 7–29.
Auden, W.H. (1940). *Collected poems* (reprinted 1968). New York, NY: Random House.
Barry, B. (1989). *Theories of justice: A treatise on social justice* (vol.1). Berkeley, CA: University of California Press.
Bion, W. (1922). *Common sense in cogitations*. London, England: Karnac.
Conrad, P. (2007). *The medicalization of society: On the transformation of human conditions into treatable disorders*. Baltimore, MD: Johns Hopkins.
Danto, E. (2006). *Freud's free clinics: Psychoanalysis and social justice*. New York, NY: Columbia University Press.
Fraiberg, S. (1959). *The magic years*. New York, NY: Charles Scribner.
Grolnick, S., Barkin, L., & Muensterberger, W. (Eds.). (1978). *Between reality and fantasy*. Northvale, NJ: Jason Aronson.
Honderich, T. (1995). *The Oxford companion to philosophy* (pp. 493–496). Oxford, England: Oxford University Press.
James, C. (2006). *Cultural amnesia: Necessary memories from history and the arts*. New York, NY: Norton.
Kristeva, J. (1997). From strangers to ourselves. In K. Oliver (Ed.), *The portable Kristeva* (pp. 264–292). New York, NY: Columbia University Press.
Layton, L., Hollander, N. C., & Gutwill, S. (2006). *Psychoanalysis, class and politics: Encounters in the clinical setting*. New York, NY: Routledge.
Leonard, P. (1997). *Postmodern welfare: Reconstructing an emancipatory project*. Thousand Oaks, CA: Sage.
Lifton, R. (1978). Advocacy and corruption in the healing profession. In C. R. Figley (Ed.), *Stress disorders among Vietnam veterans* (pp. 209–230). New York, NY: Brunner Mazel.
Lindy, J. D. (1989). Countertransference and post-traumatic stress disorder. Sihot dialogue. *Israel Journal of Psychotherapy, III*(2), 94–101.
Miller-Florshein, D. (2002). From containment to leakage, from the collective to the unique: Therapist and patient in shared national trauma. In C. Covington, P. Williams, J. Arundale, & J. Knox (Eds.), *Terrorism and war: Unconscious dynamics of political violence* (pp. 71–87). London, England: Karnac.
National Association of Social Work. (2008). *Code of ethics*. Washington, DC: Author.
Samuels, A. (1993). *The political psyche*. London, England: Karnac.
Shay, J. (1994). *Achilles in Vietnam: Combat trauma and the undoing of character*. New York, NY: Scribner.
Shay, J. (2002). *Odysseus in America: Combat trauma and the trials of homecoming*. New York, NY: Scribner.
Taylor, C. (1992). *Multiculturalism and "The politics of recognition": An essay*. Princeton, NJ: Princeton University Press.
Weber, M. (1958). *The Protestant ethic and the spirit of capitalism*. New York, NY: Charles Scribner.

Chapter 5
Virtual Intimacy in the Therapeutic Space: Help or Hindrance?

Carol Tosone

Introduction

"Should I unfriend him or just hide his posts?" asks Connie about her boyfriend who initiated their breakup following her return from an overseas vacation. "After all," she went on to say, "he didn't poke me or comment on my wall when I posted pictures of the trip. I heard from almost everyone else...Wait, I'll check again." She begins to fiddle deftly with her BlackBerry, checking texts, Facebook, and Twitter alerts, all in an effort to give her therapist an up-to-the-minute report. "No news," she says, while keeping one eye online and the other on her therapist via Skype.

This scenario is increasingly more common as clinicians, whether trained in classical Freudian psychoanalysis or contemporary cognitive behavioral therapy, are able to conduct treatment in the comfort and convenience of their homes, unbeknownst to patients they work with on Skype. Clinicians can be in New Zealand one day, Paris the next, and continue to work with patients they might have referred to another colleague when the patient moved to a different state, uninterrupted and as a matter of routine course. Are clinicians who do this avoiding the termination process? Is Connie's therapist complicit in or an active participant in her resistance to traditional treatment? Do therapists who conduct treatment via Skype, e-mail, or other technologies give new meaning to the words "acting out in the countertransference"? Is what they are doing considered ethical and in the best interests of the patient? Can work with Connie be subsumed under the rubric of psychodynamic treatment, or does it defy categorization? Or, are these therapists adapting to an ever-increasing technologically sophisticated world, one in which its citizens communicate instantaneously, candidly, and often without the counsel of an observing ego?

C. Tosone (✉)
Silver School of Social Work, New York University, New York, NY 10012, USA
e-mail: carol.tosone@nyu.edu

E. Ruderman and C. Tosone (eds.), *Contemporary Clinical Practice: The Holding Environment Under Assault*, Essential Clinical Social Work Series,
DOI 10.1007/978-1-4614-4124-3_5,

These are soul-searching questions to be pondered and debated in psychoanalytic circles such as the American Association for Psychoanalysis and Clinical Social Work (AAPCSW), the National Association of Social Workers (NASW), the American Psychoanalytic Association (APA), and other professional organizations. One's response likely depends on the timing of psychoanalytic training, current theoretical perspective, level of technological acumen, and degree of technophobia. While it is tempting to offer definitive guidelines or speak confidently about one's own approach, research on the topic of cybertherapy affirms that it is still very much a work in progress (Birke, 2008). Insurance companies, ethical boards of professional organizations, and individual practitioners are trying to determine its level of utility and whether it is a help or hindrance to the treatment process.

This chapter offers a foray into the world of cyber-treatment, complete with the state-of-the-art lexicon, applications, and research, as well as a clinician's experience as a virtual therapist. It is up to the reader to decide if cyber-treatment is psychoanalytic heresy or inevitable destiny.

Technology, Treatment, and Cybertherapy

Telephone Therapy

E-therapy is a general term used interchangeably with cybertherapy and virtual therapy to describe a variety of Internet-based treatments, including e-mail counseling, iChat, online discussion forums, videoconferencing, Skype therapy, avatar therapy, and virtual confidants (Lamb, 2004). Teleconferencing or telephone psychotherapy, a more familiar and less technologically sophisticated form of treatment, is frequently included under the rubric of e-therapy, as is text messaging.

Beginning with the most familiar and frequently used form of e-therapy, telephone therapy has been studied in relation to cognitive behavioral treatment (CBT). Carlbring and Smit (2008), for instance, compared waiting list subjects to pathological gamblers without a history of comorbid severe depression ($N=66$). They provided 8-week Internet-based CBT with minimal therapist contact via e-mail and weekly telephone calls of less than 15 minutes. Members of the experimental group evinced significant improvement in their gambling addiction, anxiety, depression, and quality of life. The Internet-based treatment effects were maintained up to 3 years. In another study, phone CBT was compared to phone-administered supportive emotion-focused therapy for depression, both 16 weeks in duration. CBT was found to be significantly more effective (Mohr et al., 2005).

Similarly, Simon, Ludman, Tutty, Operskalski, and Von Korff (2004) recruited 600 adults beginning antidepressant treatment in a primary care setting and randomly assigned them to three groups: primary care as usual, telephone care management, and telephone care management, and telephone psychotherapy. They found that 80% of depressed patients treated by telephone with 8 sessions of CBT reported a marked decline in depression symptoms, compared with 66%

of the care management group and 55% of those who got only typical primary care follow-ups. The researchers concluded that telephone psychotherapy might lack the "richness" of traditional face-to-face psychotherapy, but that it is a cost-effective, nonstigmatizing way to disseminate effective depression treatment. In a related study, Ludman, Simon, Tutty, and Von Korff (2007) found similar results comparing 8-session CBT administered by phone to primary care treatment alone for depressed patients; the researchers concluded that convenience and accessibility of empirically based telephone treatment was a viable alternative to in-person treatment.

In a study of Israeli citizens experiencing anticipatory anxiety related to potential war-related attacks, Somer, Tamir, Maguen, and Litz (2005) found that very brief CBT methods, such as breathing exercises and cognitive restructuring, could be effectively provided by paraprofessionals via the phone. As with the Simon et al. (2004) and Ludman et al. (2007), telephone-based care is a useful therapeutic medium for those who are fearful of stigma or logistically unable to access care.

Mobile Phone Therapy

Boschen and Casey (2008) surveyed the use of mobile phones for patients suffering from specific phobias. The advantage is that patients are able to contact their therapist from their current location and could complete homework tasks in vivo. They note that text messaging can be a viable substitute for phone or face contact when information needs to be exchanged and direct communication is not possible. A patient may also record an image of a feared item or animal and then use the image in psychotherapy or for homework-exposure therapy. Also, the Internet feature on a mobile phone allows the user to access therapy-based Web sites immediately or when most needed. Despite its utility for facilitating short-term, evidence-based CBT treatment, there is limited research on the clinical application of mobile devices.

Comparing Distance Technology

When comparing communication modalities, there is generally no difference in outcomes (Day & Schneider, 2002). That is, when face-to-face therapy is compared to audio and video therapies using a 5-week CBT approach, all are equally effective. Interestingly, patients were found to be more involved when using distance methods; distance created a safe space and facilitated increased openness. Importantly, most of the studies involving distance technology utilize a CBT protocol rather than a psychodynamic approach. Long-term psychoanalytic treatment does not readily lend itself to empirical comparison.

Internet-Based Treatment

As with mobile and telephone-based therapy, the empirical support for Internet-based treatment is largely CBT focused. In randomized controlled trials examining Internet-based treatment for generalized anxiety disorder (GAD; Titov, Andrews, Johnston, Robinson, & Spense, 2010) and depression (Perini, Titov, & Andrews, 2009), participants were randomly assigned to either a diagnostic-related treatment group or wait-list control group. Both treatment groups participated in an 8-week program consisting of six online lessons, access to a moderated online discussion forum, homework assignments, and weekly e-mail and telephone contact from a psychologist. Coupled with clinical guidance, the researchers for both studies concluded that Internet-based programs are effective with GAD and depression. In addition to mental health applications, Internet-based treatment can also be useful in the health arena. For example, Internet support groups have an advantage over face-to-face group therapy in that people can participate regardless of their medical situation, and the same therapeutic factors are at play (Taylor & Luce, 2003).

E-mail counseling, Web chat, and Skype are commonly used Internet-based approaches, particularly for younger therapists. Anthony, Nagel, and Gross (2010) note the popularity of these approaches with college students, members of the LGBT community, and younger therapists reared on the Internet. They find that e-mail counseling is used for clients who find writing more conducive to opening up than face-to-face meetings; a client e-mails an outline of their problem with lengthy responses from the therapist. Web chats work similarly but have the advantage of instantaneous communication. When treatment occurs through the medium of writing, clients can save their correspondence and that of the therapist, and it reduces disagreement as to what a participant in the therapeutic process actually said. Conversely, words do not convey the important visual and tonal cues to convey the intention of one's statement. Skype reduces the anonymity of e-mail but has a distinct advantage to create intimacy from a physical distance.

Virtual Therapists

In his review of the research on virtual therapeutic environments, Carey (2010) found that virtual avatars are being used successfully as therapists to treat posttraumatic stress disorder and have also been used to sensitize students to the experience of older adults. Research also suggests that dropping a young man or woman into the virtual body of an elderly person increases sympathy for the other's perspective. Researchers have experimented with different versions of virtual therapists—male, female, young, old, white, and black—all in an effort to better engage the client. For instance, at the University of Southern California, researchers found that the virtual therapist, Angelina, elicits an essential element in any therapy: self-disclosure (Kang & Gratchen, 2010, cited in Carey, 2010). People with social anxiety confessed more of their personal flaws, fears, fantasies, and traumatic experiences to virtual figures than to live therapists conducting video interviews. Sim Coach, a virtual avatar developed by this research group for the army, appears on a computer screen and can conduct a rudimentary interview, gently probing for possible mental health issues (Carey, 2010).

Ethical and Legal Considerations in the Use of Virtual Therapy

As noted previously, much of the research has been conducted in relation to CBT, leaving psychoanalytically oriented and general mental health practitioners pondering how to effectively incorporate e-therapy into their daily practices. Professional societies have been slow to address the ethics of and guidelines for virtual therapy. The APA cautions its members to be aware of ethical and legal perils, as does the Association of State and Provincial Psychology Boards. APA members are expected to review the characteristics and methods of the treatment being provided, provide confidentiality, and take into account state licensure board rules (APA, 1997). Importantly, at the present time, the NASW and the AAPCSW offer no clear guidelines.

Rehm (2008) notes the plethora of unregulated Web sites offering all forms of e-therapy, the potential violation of Health Insurance Portability Act regulations with virtual exchange of information, and the question of where the treatment takes place when a clinician resides in one state and the client in another. If there are problems warranting legal action, is the treatment considered to take place where the clinician or client resides? Does a clinician need to be licensed to practice in the state where the client is residing or only where he or she is initiating the treatment? What legal recourse does the client have if treatment is conducted internationally? Also, many insurance companies do not have established policies in regard to Skype and telephone therapy and often do not pay for e-therapy sessions. These are growing concerns yet to be fully addressed by the professional organizations, state licensing boards, and international courts.

E-therapy: A Case Illustration

From the psychoanalytic perspective, does e-therapy serve as a viable means of communication or as a resistance to therapeutic intimacy? Is e-therapy the twenty-first century version of the analyst's couch? The following case illustration is offered in an attempt to answer these questions. It should not serve as a model but as one practitioner's struggle with incorporating technology into traditional psychodynamic treatment.

Lisa is a statuesque ethnic beauty, a real head turner, in her mid-20s, who is currently studying painting in Amsterdam. Painting is her third career, the first being computer science and the second was acting. Twenty-six seems like a tender age to have had three careers, but Lisa's professional identity mirrors that of her personal life. Straight, bi, and gay were labels she eschewed as categorization and which she felt reduced one's ability to connect intimately with others.

When the therapist began working with Lisa 2 years ago in New York, she was in the midst of her acting career. She readily garnered the attention of acting coaches, fellow actors, and predatory casting directors. She had a sweet, impressionable way about her. She believed in earnest when someone said they wanted to help her career; often they just wanted to salaciously help themselves to a young actress eager to further her career in any way necessary. Untoward advances from an older, corpulent producer sent her into a tailspin, reawakening childhood memories of sexual abuse by one of her cousins.

Lisa was frustrated because she believed that her struggles with cutting and a history of bulimia were behind her. "After all," she told me, "I've been in and out of treatment for years." She recited a worn-out narrative of an older cousin who made multiple, unwelcome advances, largely from the ages of 10–12. "A real beauty," she was told again and again by him and her numerous other older cousins. Attractiveness in a Muslim culture where women were objectified and subject to Sharia law was a liability, not something desirable. A shaved head, prominent cuts, and large tattoos were ways in which she consciously protected herself. She achieved this insight in therapy, although she didn't recall with whom. "There have been so many…they all seem to melt into one therapist." She reluctantly acknowledged significant progress and was grateful that only superficial cuts were her symptom de jour.

Lisa changed therapists often in defiance of her mother who insisted Lisa needed ongoing help. So Lisa complied, each time finding some perceived fault with the therapist: a male therapist who was too seductive, an older Jewish female psychiatrist who was overmedicating her because she was Muslim, a new age therapist who was "way out there," to name just a few. As she enumerated her many treatment experiences, the therapist found her fragile narcissism and fallacious grandiosity becoming engaged. Would this therapist be the one who would make the difference, the one with whom she could relate and internalize, and the one who could help her change her internal monologue?

This was the first time she sought treatment for herself, and she had been doing relatively well on her own until this precipitant. Sessions were filled with self-doubt about her career. Did she really want to be an actress, or did it serve as another act of defiance and an attempt at autonomy? Her parents were embarrassed by her career and mindful that Lisa's grandparents disapproved of what she was doing. If Lisa would only return back to Chicago, her grandparents would buy her an apartment and car and of course fix her up with a suitable partner. Her parent and grandparents were born in Iraq and adhered to the cultural mandates. Lisa's symptoms and refusal to date Muslim men belied the appearance of a successful, model family.

Lisa alternated between a self-representation engendered by her parents and one where she saw herself as spokesperson for all that was wrong with the culture. When she saw herself as disobedient and as humiliating her family, symptoms of cutting and sexual promiscuity dominated the clinical picture. Months of treatment were devoted to helping Lisa get a better understanding of her deepest desires and helping her to fully understand the motivations for her self-destructive choices. Gradually, she came to identify herself as an artist and began to transform a hobby and unschooled talent into a career. She fought successfully for her parents' financial support and their approval for her to study abroad.

Enter Skype. With her history of acting out and gender confusion, Lisa was not an ideal candidate for Skype. She sometimes forgot sessions; it was often difficult to follow a theme; and she would frequently reference multiple partners. Lisa told the therapist that she should be flattered that she wanted to continue, and that if the therapist refused, she doubted that she would continue. Was it a compliment or blackmail? The therapist's narcissism was engaged but so was her anxiety. Absent was a sound clinical assessment or well-formulated treatment plan. What would be the treatment goals? How would the therapist compensate for the refined visual cues and in-person attunement that would be missing? Lisa's concerns were more concrete and limited to the time difference and what to do when her Internet was down. "Would it be ok if we spoke from an Internet café if we had to?" she inquired, in the event that her Internet was out. She also wanted the therapist to keep abreast of her activities by "friending" her on Facebook.

The therapist insisted that Lisa would need to take firewall precautions and make sure her roommates were not nearby; a Mac or working Webcam was a necessity, not an option. Confidentiality and the boundaries of treatment needed to be intact. Sessions were extended from 45 minutes to 1 hour to take into account the inevitable dropped sessions and poor connections. With these stipulations, weekly Skype sessions began.

Despite being a multilinguist, Lisa had a rough adjustment and felt isolated in Amsterdam. She spent the major portion of her free time on Facebook making up posts that sounded as if she was having the time of her life. "Appearance on Facebook is everything," she told her therapist, and she didn't want to disappoint her 200 listed "friends." Lisa told similar lies to her parents so that they wouldn't chide her for leaving the United States. Their doubt fueled her own, and in one of the earliest Skype sessions, she spoke about the urge to cut.

Facebook as a social medium has the potential to bridge geographical and other distances, but from a therapeutic standpoint, it also has the potential to foster pathological dissociative states. If she were sitting across from the therapist, her intent could be better intuited; the clinician could lean forward, acknowledge her psychic pain, comfort her tears, and explore the triggers. How does the therapist communicate this sentiment to a grainy talking head that is over 3,000 miles away? Was she crying? The therapist found it hard to tell from her voice. The notion of therapeutic intimacy had to be redefined, and the therapist had to bridge the physical and technological chasms between them. The clinician acknowledged being at a disadvantage and stated "it's harder to let you know that I'm with you, really with you in this. I'll need your help." The clinician then asked Lisa if she was crying. Frightened that she was over her head, the clinician offered to find Lisa a psychological resource in Amsterdam, something Lisa refused. She did agree to

Skype or e-mail if she needed to speak in-between sessions and also journal her thoughts and feelings as they occurred.

With time and in the absence of full body cues, the therapist became more adept at picking up on affective and vocal signals. Silences were more difficult to negotiate, and the therapist began to ask Lisa what she was feeling at the moment. Largely from anxiety, the therapist also found herself making more supportive comments geared toward sustaining Lisa's level of functioning. The therapist's words became louder, more emphatic, in an effort to establish her presence in this vacuous virtual space. After 1 year of Skype therapy, Lisa has progressed significantly and is pursuing an independent project about the plight of Muslim women in Iraq. She sends her therapist links to her Web site and YouTube which are viewed and discussed during the session. Gradually, the therapist also progressed in her comfort level with this medium. As Lisa has traveled around Europe on weekends, she has taken her therapist along via Skype. The therapist imagines the music in Vienna and the smell of chocolate croissants in Paris. The therapist is better able to appreciate using this medium.

Conclusion

The case of Lisa illustrates the complexity, convenience, fears, and frustrations of conducting e-therapy via Skype. While the transference and countertransference elements are present and discussed at select times, at what point would we say this treatment ceases to be psychoanalytic? As the psychoanalytic profession struggles to maintain its viability in the world of Facebook and instant messaging, the onus is on practitioners to demonstrate their necessity in a world where inner and outer realities are becoming interchangeable.

Consistent with the virtual world, these relationships are illusionary in nature. In cyberspace, the magical thinking of childhood reigns: I wish, therefore I am.

We are practicing in a world of instantaneous cyber connections that masquerade as intimacy. When clients are willing to reveal their deepest thoughts and send their raciest pictures to countless friends in cyberspace, how meaningful can those connections be? And, when one's identity can be constructed and reconstructed at will to satisfy a narcissistic urge, how intimate can those connections be? It is imperative for clinicians to find a way to harness this technology in service of therapeutic growth.

Virtual intimacy can both help and hinder the therapeutic space. It offers connection to physically challenged, resistant, and stigmatized clients, as well as those living in remote regions. It also affords the therapeutic dyad continuity in their work when one of the parties is relocating. As Lisa's case suggests, therapeutic intimacy can be maintained in person and via the Internet. There are also disadvantages in that this technology is not readily used by less-educated, indigent populations at risk; visual cues indicating a client's affective state are absent or curtailed; and severely depressed, suicidal, and psychotic clients are not considered good candidates for e-therapy.

In closing, each clinician and client needs to decide whether virtual therapy is a help or hindrance in the therapeutic process. If the state-of-the art hologram therapist "Mini-Me" is any indication, the future portends well for psychoanalysis and clinical social work. Mini-Me can only cock its head and nod and is totally reliant on a human for its comments.

References

American Psychological Association. (1997). *APA statement on services by telephone, teleconferencing, and internet*. Washington, DC: Author.

Anthony, K., Nagel, D. M., & Gross, S. (2010). *The use of technology in mental health: Applications, ethics, and practice*. Springfield, IL: Charles C. Thomas.

Birke, S. (2008). Virtual blues. *New Statesman, 137*, 21.

Boschen, M. J., & Casey, L. M. (2008). The use of mobile telephones as adjuncts to cognitive behavioral psychotherapy. *Professional Psychology: Research and Practice, 39*(5), 546–552.

Carey, B. (2010, November 23). Virtual healing for the real world. *New York Times*, p. D1.

Carlbring, P., & Smit, F. (2008). Randomized trial on internet-delivered self-help with telephone support for pathological gamblers. *Journal of Consulting and Clinical Psychology, 76*(6), 1090–1094.

Day, S. X., & Schneider, P. M. (2002). Psychotherapy using distance technology: A comparison of face-to-face, video, and audio treatment. *Journal of Counseling Psychology, 49*(4), 499–503.

Lamb, R. (2004). Bethesda-based internet therapy practitioners could be an answer for isolated and disconnected. *The Daily Record*, p. 1.

Ludman, E. J., Simon, G. E., Tutty, S., & Von Korff, M. (2007). A randomized trial of telephone psychotherapy and pharmacotherapy for depression: Continuation and durability of effects. *Journal of Consulting and Clinical Psychology, 75*(2), 257–266.

Mohr, D. C., Hart, S. L., Julian, L., Catledge, C., Honos-Webb, L., Vella, L., & Tasch, E. T. (2005). Telephone-administered psychotherapy for depression. *Archives of General Psychiatry, 62*, 1007–1014.

Perini, S., Titov, N., & Andrews, G. (2009). Clinician-assisted internet-based treatment is effective for depression: Randomized controlled trial. *Australian and New Zealand Journal of Psychiatry, 43*, 571–578.

Rehm, L. P. (2008). How far have we come in teletherapy? Comment on "telephone-administered psychotherapy. *Clinical Psychology: Science and Practice, 15*(3), 259–261.

Simon, G. E., Ludman, E. J., Tutty, S., Operskalski, B., & Von Korff, M. (2004). Telephone psychotherapy and telephone case management for primary care patients starting antidepressant treatment. *Journal of the American Medical Association, 292*(8), 935–942.

Somer, E., Tamir, E., Maguen, S., & Litz, B. T. (2005). Brief cognitive-behavioral phone-based intervention targeting anxiety about the threat of attack: A pilot study. *Behaviour Research and Therapy, 43*, 669–679.

Taylor, C. B., & Luce, K. H. (2003). Computer- and internet-based psychotherapy interventions. *Current Directions in Psychological Science, 12*(1), 18–22.

Titov, N., Andrews, G., Johnston, L., Robinson, E., & Spense, J. (2010). Transdiagnostic internet treatment for anxiety disorders: A randomized controlled trial. *Behaviour Research and Therapy, 48*, 890–899.

Chapter 6
What Happens to Confidentiality When the Government Enters the Treatment Room via the PATRIOT Act, HIPAA, and Managed Care?

Carole Bender

Introduction

The world irrevocably changed for Americans on September 11, 2001, the infamous day when terrorists hijacked three civilian airliners, crashing into and destroying the World Trade Center towers and damaging the Pentagon. The third airplane self-destructed in Pennsylvania before it could reach the White House.

What the terrorists did, however, on that day was more potent: they not only attacked our institutions, they assaulted the inner sense of security of all Americans. After so many years of feeling insulated from invasion, we could no longer feel safe. This attack on our psychological well-being has had many long-term effects, including an erosion of our constitutional right to privacy and the constitutional right to life, liberty, and the pursuit of happiness. Many of us are now so traumatized by the fear of more invasions that we have become passive participants in the erosion of these liberties, afraid to protest, speak out, or organize.

Eleven years have passed since 9/11, yet war and terrorism have escalated overseas. And the fear of terrorism in this country still survives and even thrives. As a result, the psychological well-being of individuals and families is still a vital issue, recently exacerbated by our deepening economic recession. Many of us have patients who come to us battered by these ongoing fears of terrorism and traumatized by the recent loss of jobs, homes, and health insurance. Much of this is compounded by the insufficient and at times inhumane public policies that either render individuals ineligible for healthcare insurance, or even if they are insured, many are now ineligible for services due to a preexisting condition.

As a clinical social worker, attorney, and a member of the AAPCSW National Study Group, I will address the legal and ethical issues that confront us in our daily

C. Bender (✉)
UCLA Luskin School of Public Affairs, Department of Social Welfare
Center on Child Welfare, Los Angeles, CA, USA
e-mail: Bender@publicaffairs.ucla.edu

E. Ruderman and C. Tosone (eds.), *Contemporary Clinical Practice: The Holding Environment Under Assault*, Essential Clinical Social Work Series,
DOI 10.1007/978-1-4614-4124-3_6, © Springer Science+Business Media New York 2013

work with patients/clients and/or analysands, at a time when the outside world menacingly enters our own treatment rooms.

The situation I have described makes it more vital than ever that all of us today examine both our personal and professional values and ethics in the context of our code(s) of ethic(s), and the state and federal laws, which regulate our practice of psychotherapy and the inner and outer worlds of both the patient and clinical social work therapist/analyst.

Law and Ethics in Clinical Social Work

Those of us required to take mandatory training in law and ethics for licensure in the state where we practice are painfully aware how much the law with its statutes, regulations, and case law affects our psychotherapy practice. Some of us are more comfortable with our professional code of ethics than with laws and regulations, because our code of ethics articulates for us ethical guidelines or standards of practice to be used in our direct practice with clients/patients/analysands. Our codes of ethics are written by members of our professional associations and not by judges and/or lawyers.

Codes of ethics provide us with a broad professional moral compass, which outlines such values as respecting the dignity and maximizing the self-determination of the individuals with whom we work. Furthermore, clinical social workers have a primary obligation to maintain the privacy of both current and former clients, whether living or deceased, and to maintain the confidentiality of material that has been transmitted to us in any of our professional roles. Exceptions to this occur only when there are overriding legal or professional reasons and, wherever possible, with the written permission of the person whom we are treating (Clinical Social Work Association, 2006). With every possible ethical dilemma, we must identify the social work values to be considered. Do any values conflict with each other and if yes, which social work values should take precedence?

The relationship between law and social work is more complex. At times, there is a tension between codes of ethics and laws and regulations. One sees or feels this tension in situations, which legally allow us, for example, under the Health Insurance Portability and Accountability Act (HIPAA) of 1996 regulations to share confidential patient information with other healthcare providers without prior consent from our client. Yet, our ethical codes tell us that confidential information should not be released to third parties without prior consent by the client. In this example, it is important to note that HIPAA (1996) permits rather than mandates a treating clinician to release patient healthcare information to other healthcare providers without prior patient consent. Unfortunately, for many of us who work in large healthcare settings, the sharing of healthcare information between healthcare providers is routinely done without prior patient consent. Instead, patients are given a HIPAA Notice of Privacy Practices consent form that outlines what the healthcare provider/psychotherapist is allowed to release without prior patient consent.

Another complication sometimes arises when our code of ethics states that it is ethical to do something, but the law states that the action is not legal. Additionally, when it comes to confidentiality, clinicians are expected to know whether HIPAA (1996), a federal law, trumps or preempts state law when it comes to sharing or disclosing patient information verbally or through releasing a client's medical record without prior patient consent.

The legal rule is that whichever law is more protective of patient privacy takes precedence. The difficulty is that a preemption analysis requires a paragraph-by-paragraph analysis, since sections of each law may be more protective of the privacy rights of the patient. When in doubt, consult with a competent attorney.

We are sometimes placed in the untenable position of choosing to be professionally ethical or following the letter of the law. When faced with such a decision, it is important for us to confer with our peer consultation groups or senior clinicians, as well as with an attorney knowledgeable in the practice of mental health law and professional malpractice before proceeding. Clinical peers can be helpful in exploring ethical issues as well as clinical issues with possible treatment suggestions, while an attorney can enlighten us regarding any legal issues and legal strategies. If we are in private practice, the final decision is ours, but we will have made a more informed decision with consultation rather than practicing alone. Furthermore, it is always better to consult proactively rather than retrospectively.

Creating an Ethical Attitude and an Ethical Space

It is helpful when faced with difficult clinical/ethical/legal treatment decisions to have a well-developed "ethical attitude." Such an attitude is described by Allphin (2002), in her paper "The Ethical Attitude in Psychotherapy" presented at the California Institute for Clinical Social Work 2002 Convocation, which focused on a "Dialogue on Ethics." Allphin posits that having an ethical attitude involves more than just following one's professional code of ethics or rules or the law. She elaborates that while ethical codes are needed to process dilemmas, complex experiences, and interactions, an ethical attitude is necessary "because rules and regulations do not adequately cover the dilemmas that occur in the therapeutic relationship, issues that need to be considered and struggled with that often have no clear 'right' answer" (Allphin, 2005, p. 452). Allphin introduces us to Wiener's (2001) concept of an "ethical space" which she describes as a safe container or holding environment where one can thoughtfully explore and process complex clinical, ethical, and/or legal dilemmas and issues.

Allowing ourselves to periodically enter our ethical space can be particularly helpful when we grapple with challenges such as whether we should break client confidentiality by filing a child or elder abuse report, by notifying a third party that he or she is in physical danger from our client, and by releasing information to a family member that his or her spouse is suicidal. Ethical space is also helpful when trying to decide whether to terminate treatment with a client when treatment is not progressing or when a client is no longer covered by his or her healthcare or managed healthcare plan. Other issues that may be troubling to clinicians are ongoing criminal acts by a client.

Some clinicians are now treating soldiers who have served in Iraq or Afghanistan and their families. An important question for our consideration is how to preserve confidentiality in the treatment room and at the same time protect soldiers and/or others from harm. The military environment is not focused enough on the emotional well-being of soldiers. The focus of our military appears to be to keep our country safe from terrorism and to prevent radical groups like Al Qaeda and the Taliban from assuming full control of the Iraqi and Afghanistan governments. To accomplish these goals, the military had to deploy more troops, increase soldiers' tours of duty in dangerous combat areas, and redeploy soldiers into combat duty several times. Since every soldier is needed, the emphasis has been on keeping soldiers combat ready. As of June 2008, more than 638,000 troops have been deployed to Iraq and Afghanistan more than once (Williamson & Mulhall, 2009). In the process, serious depression, PTSD, and bipolar disorder have sometimes been downplayed or ignored by commanding officers and even military mental health clinicians. There continues to be a strong stigma that attaches to soldiers who seek any type of mental health evaluation or services. Williamson & Mulhall (2009) citing the Mental Health Advisory Team (MHAT) IV Final Report Operation Iraqi Freedom 05-07 dated November 17, 2006, report that "military culture plays a significant role in this stigma; 21 percent of soldiers screening positive for a mental health problem said they avoided treatment because 'my leaders discourage the use of mental health services'" [and] "those most in need of counseling rarely seek it out" (p. 4).

It is not the least bit surprising that the military recently announced that there were more American soldier suicides in Iraq during 2008 than in any other war fought by this country. *New York Times* reporter Elisabeth Bumiller (2010) reports that "there were a record 160 active-duty Army Suicides… from Oct. 1, 2008, to Sept. 30, 2009." Colonel Elspeth Ritchie, a top army psychiatrist, told a suicide-prevention conference in January 2009 that "soldiers who have deployed to [war zones] have a higher suicide rate than soldiers who were never deployed" (Thomson, 2010, pp. 2–3).

Some clinicians will say that we must maintain confidentiality no matter what (Bollas & Sundelson, 1995). Other clinicians will say, "I have a duty to my patients which may include trying to prevent them from harming themselves or others," but California case law (*Tarasoff v. Regents of the University of California*, 1976) says:

> [Once] a therapist does in fact determine, or under applicable professional standards reasonably should have determined, that a patient poses a serious danger of violence to others, he bears a duty to exercise reasonable care to protect the foreseeable victim of that danger.

In response to pleas from many mental health organizations following the Tarasoff decision, the California legislature attempted to clarify the duty of clinicians created by the Tarasoff ruling by enacting California Civil Code Section 43.92 which says that a "psychotherapist has a duty to warn, protect and to predict only when: A patient has communicated to the psychotherapist a serious threat of physical violence against a reasonably identifiable victim or victims" (Behnke, Preis, & Bates, 1998, p. 21). Thus under the law, clinicians also have a duty to protect identifiable third parties from being seriously harmed by their clients. To add to this complexity, what happens to confidentiality if you are a clinician working in the armed services or at a VA hospital or clinic? Is your duty to your soldier/veteran client or to your employer (armed forces or VA) or to both?

Privacy, Confidentiality, and Privilege

The concepts of privacy, confidentiality, and testimonial privilege greatly affect the daily practices of mental health clinicians. While similar to each other, each word has a specific or unique meaning (Behnke et al., 1998). The concept of privacy can be viewed as the umbrella for the concepts of confidentiality and privilege. According to Wiener (2001), privacy "allows individuals to decide the manner and extent to which information about them is shared with others" (p. 433).

Confidentiality began as an ethical term or principle that governed the disclosure of information. "It is a basic ethical tenet of many professions" (Meyer & Weaver, 2006, p. 70); it is based on the individual's right to privacy, which is guaranteed by the US Constitution and by most state constitutions (Behnke et al., 1998), and it is the "cornerstone of effective psychotherapy" (Luepker, 2003, p. 44) as it goes to the heart of the therapeutic relationship. When therapists/analysts are able to keep client communications confidential from disclosure to unauthorized third parties, they demonstrate that they value the concept of confidentiality and respect the client's right to privacy. This helps both the therapist and the client to form and maintain a therapeutic alliance in a safe holding environment. A client's communication to a therapist cannot be revealed to third parties *unless* the therapist is legally compelled to do so (Behnke et al., 1998).

What happens to the patient's expectation of privacy when the government enters the treatment room through mandated child abuse and elder abuse reporting laws, managed care requests for client records, use of "required" forms to assess a patient's progress for substance abuse and mental health problems, and the permissive release and sharing of client mental health records without patient consent under HIPAA (1996) and the procurement of client records by the US government as permitted by Section 215 of the USA PATRIOT Act (2001)? Some would argue that this reflects an erosion of our legal right to privacy as well as erosion in the law protecting confidentiality between patients and therapists.

When it comes to patient/client confidentiality, what once *seemed* absolute is now replete with exceptions. Law students learn the general rule of law and then quickly learn to identify all exceptions to the general rule of law. As explained in the paragraphs above, exceptions to the general rule on confidentiality are the mandatory reporting statutes requiring therapists to report a reasonable suspicion of child abuse, elder or dependent abuse, or a threat to seriously harm a readily identifiable third party or parties.

Informed Consent

Because of the growing exceptions to confidentiality, it is both legally and ethically important for clinicians to inform clients at the beginning of treatment verbally and/or in writing about mandatory reporting laws and the limitations of patient/therapist confidentiality. A patient should never be surprised about mandatory reporting laws. This is sometimes referred to as "The Law of No Surprises" by attorneys (Behnke et al., 1998). Some clinicians argue that the mandatory reporting laws discourage the very people who are in need of treatment from seeking treatment. For those already in treatment, reporting laws can put a chill on patient/therapist communication.

Managed Care, Confidentiality, and Informed Consent

Another area of concern for clinicians is managed care, which has been with us in one form or another since the early 1970s. While some of us have opted out of involvement with managed care companies, some of us have chosen to be on managed care panels. It looks as if managed care is here to stay in one form or another.

So the question for all of us is how much patient information can be protected from dissemination to managed care or other health insurance plans? The lawyer in me responds with an "it depends" answer. If patients request us to bill their insurance companies, or if they have been referred to us by their HMO's because we are on an HMO panel and the patient wants his or her HMO or other healthcare insurer to pay for services, then the insurer is entitled to receive patient information such as symptoms, dates of service, diagnosis, tests performed, prescribed medications, treatment modalities and frequency of treatment, treatment plan, and prognosis. The insurer is not entitled to the patient's protected health information (PHI) often located in the therapist's psychotherapy notes under the provisions of HIPAA (1996).

In order to protect patient/therapist confidentiality, psychotherapy notes must be maintained separately from the rest of the patient's file. It is much easier for therapists in private practice to do this than it is for therapists who work in hospitals and clinics, where a therapist's psychotherapy notes are not routinely maintained separately from the rest of the patient's chart or medical record. Therefore, a clinician needs to be extremely careful about the breadth and depth of information documented in hospital and/or clinic records. It should be noted, however, that even psychotherapy notes that are kept in separate files might be discoverable in certain legal proceedings.

As much as we want to protect the confidentiality of our client's communications to us, the reality is that no records are immune from disclosure and patients need to be aware of this through the informed consent process. The informed consent process starts at the beginning of therapy and continues throughout treatment when the need arises.

The Psychotherapist-Patient Privilege and Testimonial Privilege

Testimonial privilege is a legal term, which also flows from the same values of privacy and individual autonomy; it is "the patient's right to keep confidential communications from being disclosed in a legal proceeding" (Behnke et al., 1998, p. 23).

A patient's confidentiality in legal proceedings is usually protected in courts by the psychotherapist-patient privilege, which is codified in states' evidence codes. All 50 states have some type of psychotherapist-patient privilege. Some states recognize all mental health clinicians as having this privilege, while other states may exclude licensed clinical social workers or licensed marriage family therapists from this privilege.

Prior to 1996, no psychotherapist-patient privilege existed in federal courts.

The US Supreme Court in *Jaffee v. Redmond* (1996) established the psychotherapist-patient privilege in federal courts. The court decision affirmed that therapists—including social workers—cannot be compelled to testify in federal court about communications from their client made in the course of therapy nor compelled to disclose their treatment notes in court unless their client has waived their confidentiality. What was not decided in *Jaffee v. Redmond* was whether the patient-psychotherapist privilege was absolute or whether it was subject to exceptions such as the dangerous patient exception. The federal district courts are split on this issue.

Confidentiality and the USA PATRIOT Act (Section 215)

The original USA PATRIOT Act (2001) was passed by both houses of Congress 45 days after September 11, 2001, to provide law enforcement "enhanced investigative tools" to "assist in the prevention of future terrorist activities and the preliminary acts and crimes which further such activities" (H.R. 107-236, pt. 1, at 41). Concerns then arose regarding the balance between national security issues and individual citizens' civil liberties. "Perhaps in response to such concerns, Congress established sunset provisions which apply to Sections... and Section 215 of the USA PATRIOT ACT" (Liu, 2011, p. 1). These sunset provisions have been renewed several times since 2005. Sections... and Section 215 were set to expire on May 27, 2011. However on May 26, 2011, "the three provisions were extended four approximately four years, until June 1, 2015". (Liu, 2011, p.2).

I would like to focus my discussion on Section 215, since this section can directly affect confidentiality and the psychotherapist-patient privilege. Section 215 of the USA PATRIOT Act (2001) "expanded the Foreign Intelligence Surveillance Act's (FISA) 'business records' authority" (Brand, 2010). Specifically, Section 215 "authorizes the production of 'any tangible things'" including books, records, papers, documents, and other items such as medical and psychotherapy records. "It also lowered the standard required before a court order may be issued to compel their production" (Liu, 2011, p. 9). Section 106(b) of the USA PATRIOT Improvement and Reauthorization Act of 2005 amended FISA procedures for obtaining business records by requiring the government to supply a "statement of facts showing that there are reasonable grounds to believe that the tangible things sought are relevant to a [foreign intelligence, international terrorism, or espionage investigation]."

Of concern to therapists is that the 2005 amended Section 215 (USA PATRIOT Improvement and Reauthorization Act) still allows federal agents to gain access to confidential client records without showing probable cause of a crime. Amended Section 215 also prohibits recipients (including therapists) from disclosing to clients and others that the Federal Bureau of Investigation (FBI) "has sought or obtained any tangible things pursuant to a FISA order" (Liu, 2011, p. 11). However, amended Section 215 permits recipients to discuss the order with persons needed to comply with the order, for example, an attorney, or with other persons as permitted by the FBI (50 U.S.C. Section 1861(d)(1) (2008)). Under Section 215, the recipient must reveal, if requested by the FBI, the names of all persons to whom disclosure was made except the names of any attorneys consulted (Liu, 2011, p. 11). Thus, Section 215 prohibits a therapist from revealing to his or her client that the therapist was ordered to produce the client's psychotherapy records to the FBI.

Of particular concern to us all is the apparent conflict between Section 215 of the PATRIOT Act (2001) and the required protection of confidentiality through psychotherapist-patient privilege and our professional codes of ethics. Section 215 of the PATRIOT Act is an excellent example of the law requiring us *not* to disclose to our clients that the government has requested and/or obtained their psychotherapy records. At the same time our professional code of ethics, for example, National Association of Social Workers (NASW) Code of Ethics, Standard 1.07 (e) (1999), requires a social worker to discuss with a client "the nature of confidentiality and limitations of clients' right to confidentiality." Additionally, Standard 1.07 (d) states that "social workers should discuss with clients to the extent possible, about the disclosure of confidential information and the potential consequences when feasible before the disclosure is made. This applies whether social workers disclose confidential information on the basis of a legal requirement or client consent."

Thus, a social worker with an ethical attitude, who believes strongly in protecting client confidentiality, may be faced with a situation in which the government is requesting his or her client's psychotherapy records under Section 215 of the USA PATRIOT Act (2001), yet obeying this law goes against our professional ethics. We either have to disobey the law or violate our professional code of ethics. Given the broad powers of Section 215, which allows the federal government to "seize" patient records without prior patient consent, clinicians need to seriously consider informing their patients about the USA PATRIOT Act during the informed consent process. This may be clinically contraindicated when treating paranoid people who already believe that the government is after them.

My recommendation is that any clinician who receives a USA PATRIOT Act (2001) request for confidential client documents should immediately consult with an attorney knowledgeable about social work/psychology confidentiality issues. NASW (2004) makes a similar recommendation to social work clinicians and also advises social workers to discuss the potential conflicts with their state licensing board attorney.

Conclusion

In this age of global terrorism, a worldwide deepening recession, and the increased use of technology to gather and store personal, business, and medical information about us, there is a growing concern in the United States regarding the protection of our right to privacy. In the mental health field, there is an additional concern about the protection of confidentiality with respect to what happens between patient and therapist in the treatment room.

This chapter has focused on the effect of certain laws such as HIPAA (1996) and the USA PATRIOT Act (2001) on patient confidentiality in the treatment room and of testimonial privilege in the courtroom. It has also focused on the tension that sometimes exists between law and ethics and the need for therapists to have an ethical attitude and create an ethical space when dealing with complex legal–ethical–clinical patient issues.

Given the fact that it is becoming more difficult to keep the government out of the treatment room, I would urge all of us to join and to support the advocacy of our professional organizations. And for those of us who are drawn to political activism, I urge you to become leaders in our professional organizations or groups such as the Patient Privacy Rights group, Psychotherapists for Social Responsibility, and the American Civil Liberties Union.

References

Allphin, C. (2002). *The ethical attitude.* Paper presented at the California Institute for Clinical Social Work Convocation Ethics, Studio City, CA.

Allphin, C. (2005). An ethical attitude in the analytic relationship. *Journal of Analytical Psychology, 50*, 451–468.

Behnke, S., Preis, J., & Bates, R. (1998). *The essentials of mental health law.* New York, NY: W.W. Norton.

Bollas, C., & Sundelson, D. (1995). *The new informants: Betrayal of confidentiality in psychoanalysis and psychotherapy.* London, England: Karnac Books.

Brand, R. (2010, January 20). Reauthorization of the USA PATRIOT Act. *The Federalist Society.* http://www.fed-soc.org/publications/pubid.1651

Bumiller, E. (2010, July 29). Pentagon report places blame for suicides. *The New York Times.* http://www.nytimes.com

Clinical Social Work Association. (2006). Code of ethics. *CSCSW Clinical Update* (December 2003, p. 2). http://www.clinicalsocialworkassociation.org/about-us/ethics-code

Health Insurance Portability and Accountability Act of 1996, P.L.104-191.

Jaffee v. Raymond, 518 US. 1; 1996 U.S. LEXIS 3879 (1996).

Liu, E. (2011). Amendments to the Foreign Intelligence Surveillance Act (FISA) Extended until June1, 2015. Washington, DC: Congressional Research Service Report. http://www.fas.org/sgp/crs/intel/R40138.pdf

Luepker, E. T. (2003). *Record keeping in psychotherapy & counseling.* New York, NY: Brunner-Routledge.

Mental Health Advisory Team (MHAT) IV, Final report: Operation Iraqi Freedom 05-07, November 17, 2006. http://www.armymedicine.army.mil/reports/mhat_iv/MHAT_IVReport_17NOV06.pdf

Meyer, R. G., & Weaver, C. M. (2006). *Law and mental health: A case-based approach*. New York, NY: Guilford.

National Association of Social Work. (1999). *Code of ethics*. Washington, DC: Author.

National Association of Social Work. (2004, September). NASW legal issue of the month: Social workers and the USA Patriot Act. http://www.socialworkers.org/Idf/legal_issue/2004/400409.asp?print+1&

Tarasoff v. Regents of the University of California, 17 Cal. 3d 425; 551 (P.2d 334 1976).

Thomson, M. (2010, April 13). Is the U.S. Army losing its war on suicide? *TIME*. http//www/time.com/nation/article/0,8599,1981284,00html

USA PATRIOT Act of 2001, P.L. 105-107 (2001); H.R. 107-236, pt.1 at 42 (2001).

USA PATRIOT IMPROVEMENT AND REORGANIZATION Act of 2005, Public Law 109-177, Section 106(b) (2006).

Wiener, J. (2001). Confidentiality and paradox: The location of ethical space. *Journal of Analytic Psychology, 46*(3), 431–442.

Williamson, V., & Mulhall, E. (2009, January). *Invisible wounds: Psychological and neurological injuries confront a new generation of veterans* (Iraq and Afghanistan Veterans of America, Issue Report). New York: IAVA.

Chapter 7
A Perfect Storm: The Influence of Outside Forces on Social Work Education

Barbara Berger

What differentiates the psychoanalytically informed social worker is the experience of graduate study in social work with its unique roots in the influence of environment and the biopsychosocial experience (Simpson, Williams, & Segall, 2007). And, social work education has historically balanced the value of practice experience and the academic tradition to generate the well-informed and well-trained clinician. First-year MSW students at Loyola University, Chicago School of Social Work, are taught the concept of holon: an entity that is itself a whole while simultaneously being a part of a larger whole. For example, our psychoanalytic theories become integrated with social work's roots as they are overlaid upon the knowledge of an individual as part of a family, a family that is part of a community, etc.

This same concept applies at a more macro-level, that of the graduate school of social work. Who comes to our graduate schools? Our students are individuals who care about humanity, who want to help, and who travel many paths toward the ends that social work offers. The student becomes part of the graduate program, itself a whole and also a part of the university, which is part of academia nationally. Academia is infused with the culture surrounding it, including its politics and its passions. And so, the culture influences academia, which affects the universities that comprise it, and the response of the universities influences the departments within it. Graduate schools of social work are fertile soil for such influences because they are highly sensitized by their core values as well as their needs to survive, indeed thrive, amid the dynamics within and around the universities. In the last decade, political events, cultural and economic shifts, and divisions within the social work community itself have had a major impact on social work education.

B. Berger (✉)
The Institute for Clinical Social Work, Chicago, IL 60602, USA
e-mail: bbergerphd@sbcglobal.net

E. Ruderman and C. Tosone (eds.), *Contemporary Clinical Practice: The Holding Environment Under Assault*, Essential Clinical Social Work Series,
DOI 10.1007/978-1-4614-4124-3_7, © Springer Science+Business Media New York 2013

Political Influences

In 2001, following the traumatic events of 9/11, concerns about academic freedom became a central focus for colleges and universities nationwide. A belief in the importance of academic freedom took hold firmly after McCarthyism was defeated (Streb, 2006). But, legislation like the USA PATRIOT Act (2001) seemed to threaten its continuation. Streb (2006) cites a study by the University of Illinois in 2001–2002 that stated, "…550 libraries had received requests from federal and state law-enforcement agencies for the records of patrons" (p. 9). People wondered if second thought should be given to books one bought or borrowed. In schools, governments increased their efforts at surveillance, and watchdog groups arose. These led to the denouncing of professors who spoke against the "War on Terror" or who criticized former President Bush's policies in Iraq (Streb, 2006). Fear of terrorism and concern about foreign enemies were exacerbated by fear of one's own government. As the cultural value of control increased, the educational environment became characterized by a pervasive fear from within and without.

Caution seemed the better part of valor causing teachers and students alike to be careful about their words until the political climate began to shift and come around full circle. Eventually, it became acceptable to criticize the government, but less so to support it. Was this a better situation? Not really, it is the same situation in reverse. Perhaps what seems most politically correct at any given time is only a rationalization for the censorship of disparate views.

In academia, even the perception of academic freedom and its boundaries grew controversial. Some, known as civil libertarians, believed that teachers should not be held to standards outside of their profession; professors and schools should be insulated from any political interference (Shiell, 2006). Others, speaking from a more egalitarian position, felt that the cause of equality in education was compelling enough to justify restrictions on academic life. It was this belief system that gave rise to speech codes in an attempt to legislate restrictions (Shiell, 2006), ostensibly to avoid offending any minority group.

In the most extreme position, legal moralists supported the notion that teachers, as public servants, were responsible to the taxpayers whose taxes funded schools and paid salaries. This group believed in the right of the community to appoint authorities, decide curriculum, and set rules for both teachers and students. According to Shiell (2006), the legal moralist position was that "…public education should be subject to strict moral and legal constraints which frequently override the pursuit and dissemination of knowledge in an environment of free inquiry" (p. 25). The natural, though perhaps unintended, consequence of this position is that the dominant political climate can control public education at all levels.

Universities, though, are and have been interested in preserving academic freedoms, especially as political situations change. Therefore, while attempts at restrictions have given way in schools at all levels, it is especially true in higher education. Teachers maintain the same rights to free expression as other citizens (Shiell, 2006). Because of the recognition that knowledge is best pursued in an atmosphere of free inquiry, schools generally permit a full range of debate and opinion. There is no organized effort to prevent or disallow disagreement. This freer atmosphere generates a new question and another tension. Are the rights of students to academic freedom any less important than those of their professors? This inquiry led to the birth of a group called the Students for Academic Freedom, an organization that urges schools to adopt an academic bill of rights (Magna Publications, 2004).

This group generates student clubs composed of members seeking more academic freedom by lobbying legislators and tracking occurrences of incidents based on perceived bias and intellectual diversity. A number of universities have offered support or are considering the issue. Student governments at University of California, Davis; University of Montana; Utah State University; and Brown University have asked for a student bill of rights guaranteeing academic freedom. Faculty at the University of Denver have already voted to support such a bill, and others like Emory, Grinnell, Brandeis, Georgia Tech, Tufts, and Bentley are in discussions around the issue. More schools, like Brown and Brooklyn College, teach the concept of intellectual diversity within their diversity programming (Magna Publications, 2004).

Though universities are interested in defending, perhaps even expanding the concept of academic freedom, the idea faces several obstacles in the twenty-first century. These challenges include national security, reliance on corporate funding, the increased use of nontenured teachers, and political correctness.

Of the factors influencing academic freedom, political correctness may be the most important. It is an especially crucial problem in schools of social work immersed as they are in issues of social justice, tolerance, and diversity. When political correctness dominates, it can permeate classrooms and sabotage open discussion. If we understand that words and language shape the world as we know it, then speech becomes an action with intentionality built into it. The words we choose, the language we use, can be empowering or subjugating. The development of hate speech codes was an early attempt to struggle with this problem. These codes reached a peak in the early 1990s when there were more than 300 universities that adopted such rules. Schools were making a concerted effort to ban any conduct, whether oral, written, or behavioral, that was directed against any person or group having the effect of creating offense, being intimidating, or creating a hostile environment (Uelman, 1992).

The complexity of issues became increasingly apparent as the line between the right to freedom of speech was threatened by rules protecting people's rights not to be denigrated, threatened, or harassed. In 1991, Nadine Shore, then President of the American Civil Liberties Union, said that while racial incidents and bias were troubling, speech codes were an unacceptable and unconstitutional way of dealing with them. Others defended the need for these codes in order to make education without terror and intimidation accessible to all students. The courts, however, disagreed with this effort and began to strike down these regulations based on their violation of constitutional rights (Hartman, 1991).

While all this is happening within schools, and between schools and the courts, there are other disputes simmering as people are affected by the changing cultural and political milieu of the country. Tensions build as the interface of pressure from within the university meets the demands of the external world. Friction and hostility escalate when particular professional values, like concerns about social justice and human rights in social work education, become challenges to the freedom of an individual's right to choose her or his own beliefs. This debate further intensifies with shifts and changes in the current political environment. Since 9/11, our culture has grown increasingly to become one imbued with fear and mistrust. The objects of our fears may alter, but they still exist. In the United States, we have elected an African-American as President, Barack Obama, and have more women in positions of power, but others are now the objects of discrimination.

Nowhere does the complexity of the issue and the need to struggle for better solutions become more powerful than in education and most particularly social work education. It is in this arena that a balance must be found between the discomforts that are tolerable for the protection of freedom of speech and limitations creating boundaries preventing interference with the rights of others. As we "sort principle from sentiment" (Pelton, 2001), it becomes apparent that "offense" is not sufficient for the institution of prohibitions—actually, everything or anything can, potentially, offend someone. And, rules against using language that reflects bias can create a sense of censorship based on political correctness. But then, how and when do we impose restrictions? When does "free" go too far? Longres (1994) said, "Rules against bias may also have the effect of turning us into spin doctors…" (p. 284). The situation compels the search for answers to certain questions:

Do students limit their participation or areas of study because of political correctness?
Do they report discomfort and self-censorship in the selection of courses?
Is political correctness the reason for self-censorship among students?

Hyde and Ruth (2002) conducted research concerning these issues among a student population at Boston University School of Social Work. Their conclusions were that although factors like shyness and general class preparation were major issues, factors concerning political correctness and the opinions of peers and instructors were significant. It's interesting that the researchers noted students attributed such concerns to their peers more than to themselves. We might think in terms of the need for students to project their own worries about being misperceived onto others in order to avoid feeling poorly judged themselves.

Pelton (2001) refers to social justice as the mission of social work, but he notes that its definition may be based on biased data. The Counsel on Social Work Education (CSWE) requires courses on racism, social justice, and others because we are a value-laden profession with a long-standing commitment to social justice issues (Hartman, 1991). This is why social work educators, perhaps with even more sensitivity than others, must struggle and debate these issues. This field has a most unique problem in finding an acceptable balance.

Our discipline is committed to the relief of the impoverished and the persecuted and the disabled and needy. The very history of social work has its roots in advocating for the poor and underprivileged. This certainly leads to a pervasive, discipline-wide concern for the importance of a social justice focus (Hartman, 1991; Pelton, 2001).

The growing atmosphere of fear and mistrust that has come to characterize American culture exacerbates such a concern. While it seems that for the past decade our society has grown less tolerant and more polarized in its views, schools of social work have tried to hold fast to their professional values. The result of the desire to embrace multiculturalism, diversity, and difference has been an increased urgency for the use of politically correct language, which can create limits to academic freedom and thought for students and faculty (Hyde & Ruth, 2002). Perhaps for social work, it seems oxymoronic to think about "tolerable offenses." But, correspondingly, perhaps we disenfranchise the rights of one group when we privilege the rights of another.

This conundrum has, unfortunately, led to the perception that schools of social work are an exception to the movement in universities toward the preservation of academic freedom, perhaps for both teachers and students. It is paradoxical that a group so concerned with insight about fairness and the needs of others should be so unaware of its own intolerance, its own discriminatory practices. These contradictions are significant and a closer look is required.

In the spring of 2007, the National Association of Scholars (NAS) conducted a study of ten schools of social work in public universities, later published under the headline of "The Scandal of Social Work Education." They categorize these schools as top ranked, a determination based on enrollment statistics and the availability of the information necessary for the study posted on the Web sites of the universities. NAS reviewed accreditation standards, standards for student assessment, each school's own definition of itself, and program objectives, mission statements, and descriptions of course content. Not surprisingly, they discovered that CSWE's Educational and Policy Standards included words implying advocacy and activism as part of the social work job description.

Rather than presenting a professional value, the words in the document take a left political position and, as such, are imbued with ideology. NAS (2007) concluded that such biased emphasis on social justice left no place for alternative views in academics. This single viewpoint, couched in clear political terminology, promotes a prejudice in the approach toward helping the poor and needy. It leaves no room for debate or discussion of other ideas, or in some cases, even alternate beliefs about methodologies that might be helpful. CSWE, as the national accreditation organization, encourages, perhaps even requires, schools to institute policies for mandatory student advocacy (NAS, 2007).

David Stoesz (2008), professor of social work at Virginia Commonwealth University, accuses CSWE of creating a spoils system in professional education at the public expense. He even goes so far as to suggest that because CSWE, in an attempt to live by its own principles, requires representation by members of underrepresented groups on its own Board, they have grown increasingly mired in identity politics, sacrificing representation of the most scholarly. He claims CSWE has created an "academic cocoon in which patronage regularly trumps merit" (Stoesz, 2008). Perhaps this is another example of the law of unintended consequences causing unforeseen challenges. It is a well-intentioned idea run amuck.

CSWE (2007) vehemently disagreed with the conclusions of the NAS (2007) study and responded with a letter to its own membership:

> The mission of CSWE is to provide quality assurance for social work education programs as they prepare professionals for social work practice based on the profession's history, purposes, philosophy, and body of knowledge, values and skills. It is incumbent upon the individual programs and their faculties to develop appropriate educational formats and curricula within their institutional contexts for the education of social work practitioners…The profession itself has a long and time-honored practice tradition of advocacy for social justice as well as a commitment to participation and inclusion in the structures of democratic society. Fundamental to social justice is the protection of individual and academic freedom of thought and expression, including religious and political beliefs. Social work education, through the CSWE accreditation process, expects social work faculty and students to respect diversity of thought and practice in the pursuit of social justice and in the academic context that reflects the program's mission and purpose. (CSWE, 2007)

The commission continues its defense against accusations made by the NAS (2007) study and an article printed in the *Washington Post* by George Will (2007) that contended "that social work education and practice are devoid of critical thinking and balanced analysis." CSWE insists that it requires social work programs to prepare graduates to "apply critical thinking skills within the context of professional social work practice" (CSWE, 2007).

It seems that CSWE intends to guarantee students the right to be independent thinkers, as long as they have respect for the history, philosophy, and values of the social work profession.

The interweaving of CSWE's (2008) Educational Policy and Accreditation Standards (EPAS) with National Association of Social Worker's (NASW) Code of Ethics (1999) may complicate the unintentional constriction of a student's potential for critical thinking and freedom to apply personal moral or religious values. In a document that explains the function and intent of the EPAS (CSWE, 2008), entitled "Purpose: Social Work Practice, Education, and Educational Policy and Accreditation Standards," Section 2.1.2 on values and ethics specifically states, "Social workers make ethical decisions by applying standards of the National Association of Social Workers Code of Ethics." Section 1.1 states of the 2008 EPAS (CSWE), "Service, social justice, the dignity and worth of the person, the importance of human relationships, integrity, competence, human rights, and scientific inquiry are among the core values of social work." The document states that the first six in this list reflect the NASW Code of Ethics (1999).

NASW's Code of Ethics (1999) is a lengthy document covering many aspects of professional ethics. But it definitely underscores the imperative of promoting social justice with advocacy in many of its sections. Specifically, in Section 6.01, the code (NASW, 1999) states, "social workers should advocate for living conditions conducive to the fulfillment of basic human needs and promote social, economic, and political institutions that are compatible with the realization of social justice." In other sections, the code uses similar left, liberal rhetoric enjoining social workers to "engage in social and political action" and "advocate for changes in policy and legislation to improve social conditions to meet basic human needs and promote social justice" (NAS, 2007). Clearly, the NASW (1999) code shares the CSWE (2008) ideological stance as well as the demand for advocacy. It can, therefore, become a covert impingement on self-determination and individual belief systems.

Will, in his 2007 article "The *Code of Coercion*," referred to the social work Code of Ethics (NASW, 1999), approved in 1996 and revised in 1999 by the NASW Delegate Assembly, as a surreptitious political agenda. He quotes a social work textbook, still popular in schools at this time, *Direct Social Work Practice: Theory and Skill*. The text is supportive of the obligatory nature of the message to students in the NASW code. Will (2007) quotes, "social and economic justice is especially imperative as a response to the conservative trends of the past three decades." Clearly, this language alters a value of the profession and, with a political turn, veers onto a slippery slope of mandating opinion, a predetermined judgment of that which is good.

The NAS (2007) study noted that the mission statements of the schools reflected adherence to the political ideology of social justice advocacy, and nine of the ten schools studied required students to endorse the NASW (1999) code as a condition of graduation. The ideology is repeated in handbooks and field manuals and in course descriptions and penetrates the classroom. For example, at Arizona State University, students must "demonstrate compliance with the NASW Code of Ethics." At University of California, Berkeley, compliance is considered proof of "suitability for the profession," and at the University of Michigan, failure to comply may be considered "academic misconduct" (Streb, 2006). At UCLA, a core course syllabus says, students are "required to view the 'Primetime: Racism/Discrimination' video that complements the week 1 lecture on White Privilege" (NAS, 2007).

The issue about which to be concerned is not whether any of us agrees or disagrees with the basic value of our profession concerning social justice and the well-being of all people. Rather, it is to propose that even a position advocating for what we believe is good can become so legislated, so rigidified, that it impinges on the freedom of individuals to think, to speak, or to act in accordance with their own value systems. Although, initially a reaction to shifts in social changes, when the insistence on prescribed forms of advocacy become too absolute, they become no less restrictive and dictated than any other form of fundamentalism. At that point, we become that which we mean to oppose.

The NAS (2007) study asserts that "No college or university, and most certainly not public ones can properly demand that a student publicly affirm a particular ideology or political position, much less engage in overt advocacy on its behalf." Advocacy is a fine concept deserving of attention, but the report (NAS, 2007) exclaims, "In higher education, advocacy can sometimes be welcomed as a passenger, but has no right to take the wheel." The distinction between instruction and indoctrination is a line that must be respected.

The example of Emily Brooker, social work student at Missouri State University (MSU), provides a poignant instance in which the line was blurred. In a required course on social welfare policy and services, the teacher assigned a semester-long compulsory project. Students were to write papers advocating for the rights of homosexuals to provide foster homes and to become adoptive parents. This was to be followed by the class drafting a letter to the Missouri state legislature on MSU stationary urging legislation in favor of homosexual adoption to be signed by every student (NAS, 2007).

Ms. Brooker approached her professor and her advisor with objections based on her feeling that this assignment violated her religious beliefs. With some reluctance, the professor permitted her to pick a different project. However, just before the final exam for the course, Ms. Brooker received notification that she was charged with the most serious, level 3, violation of ethical standards. A 2-h hearing in front of a panel of seven faculty, from which her parents were excluded and during which no recording could be made, was held to focus on a charge of "discriminatory conduct" for refusing to sign the letter to the legislature. The decision held that Emily Brooker should write a paper explaining her work to "lessen the gap" between her personal ethics and the professional ethics of social work. Not only was she required to present this paper to a group of faculty but she had to state that she would not discriminate against homosexuals and would be willing to place children in homosexual adoptive homes. They further demanded that she sign a paper committing to the NASW Code of Ethics and the School Standards. Following her graduation, in 2006, Ms. Brooker filed a civil rights action and sued the school. A settlement was made in which she was cleared of charges and awarded financially; MSU did a self-evaluation, and the professor stepped down from his post (NAS, 2007).

The experiences of William Felkner provide an example of a student who identified himself as a political conservative at Rhode Island College, School of Social Work. He was assigned a course project to lobby the Rhode Island legislature on proposed measures relating to social welfare policy. Mr. Felkner resisted because he opposed the expansion of government advocated in these propositions. Instead, he attempted to write a paper presenting his own conservative political views but was given a failing grade in the course. His project was finally approved, and he was assigned a professor but encountered such obstruction and hostility to his work that his graduation was seriously threatened. Mr. Felkner filed a discrimination suit against the school in 2006, 2 years after he entered, for penalizing his grades, ridiculing him, delaying his graduation, and preventing him from working on welfare reform in the governor's office. In 2008, the college filed a summary judgment, which was denied by the court. Settlement negotiations continue to be in process (NAS, 2007).

If the profession of social work espouses the need for respect for all individuals, doesn't it need to respect the social justice principles of nondiscrimination among themselves as well as in the world at large? As schools teach about the dangers of participation in coercive political systems leading to the process of selection and exclusion, there must be a reflective, insightful caution about the need to avoid the politics of group identity, the "we/they," among ourselves. Leroy Pelton (2001), Chair of the Child Welfare Concentration in the MSW Program at University of Nevada, Las Vegas, calls for education to reflect about complicity with unfair systems. If, as Pelton states, "treating individuals in the same circumstances in the same way is the essence of non-discrimination" (p. 433), does that not apply within the educational system as well as outside of it?

Might it not be useful to debate the subjects of multiculturalism and the celebration of ethnic alliances vs. the value of encouraging assimilation or the cause of poverty as oppression vs. the need to promote individual efforts? Shouldn't we encourage Mr. Felkner and our own selves to "make the world a better place" by understanding the complexity of issues on all sides of the social policy issue? And, might Ms. Brooker's learning be better served by asking her to write her paper as an exercise in understanding the arguments on both sides of the same sex adoption issue, rather than attempting to force her to adhere to a political position by signing a petition? It seems that different people with different ideas bring richness to the profession as long as there is an ability to understand and work with others of varying beliefs. The capacity to be empathic, to embrace difference, and to be tolerant as we work with others of different mindsets—these are professional ideals. Tolerance of difference, after all, is what ultimately invites true social justice.

John Stuart Mill argues that closing access to ideas leads to the assumption that there is certainty, but such certainty is not possible (Shiell, 2006). While most views have some portion of truth in them, it is the integration of ideas that leads to the most truth. Alternative viewpoints always enrich meaning, even in the face of a generally accepted opinion. Without other views, there grows the danger of developing prejudice or dogma (Shiell, 2006). After 9/11, the belief was that one should only speak in support of the "War on Terror." Anything else was unpatriotic (Streb, 2006). This is no less dogmatic than the tidal wave of opinion against Bush and the war in which those who disagree are silenced by the accusation of being warmongers.

Pelton (2001) says, "...a just community must be one that benefits all of its individuals without discrimination, and social work must be concerned with promoting such a community" (p. 433). In the CSWE (2007) letter in response to the NAS (2007) study, it is acknowledged that "Fundamental to social justice is the protection of individual and academic freedom of thought and expression, including religious and political beliefs." Because it is important for people to feel that they are unbiased and objective, defenses allow the denial of bias and/or a sense of justification. As the political scene has changed, as politics have influenced thinking, values that were once based on the long-standing social work traditions of service, the value of human dignity, and the cause of social justice may have become rigidified. It is this rigidity that leads to judgmental attitudes and pejorative behaviors.

The profession and the associations representing social work must insist on the intolerance of intolerance. But, our programs continue to change as outside influences multiply with complex issues arising in local contexts as well as the national scene.

Economic Influences

As impassioned political tides continue to affect schools of social work across the country, economic issues simultaneously create enormous pressures on the system. The need for funds has driven changes in the selection of faculty and, ultimately, has generated a number of contentious splits in the academic community. While all universities insist on excellence in teaching as a priority, the value that practice informs teaching and research is losing its historic status as a basic truth in social work education. In an attempt to professionalize the profession, more and more tenure-track faculty are being hired directly out of doctoral programs because they have published and done research and are more likely to be able to bring in grant money for the school (Johnson & Munch, 2010). This is true despite the fact that many doctoral students have little practice experience.

In my experience, colleagues report that faculty members established in teaching positions are under constantly increasing pressure to publish and present, or be considered as lacking. In some cases, extra teaching is added as a consequence of insufficiency in the number of publications, making it seem as if teaching is a penalty. Teaching values and quality are effectively sacrificed to the emphasis on research grants and publications. Thus, the number of tenured faculty who have practice backgrounds is shrinking as other priorities and job requirements take precedence. Many schools of social work have fewer than 20 % of their tenure/tenure-track faculties with practice backgrounds. This shift may have its greatest impact on the experience of the students.

While the ranking of candidate choices for tenure-track positions is influenced by dollars, there is clearly a devaluing of clinical practice. The tension grows as a dialogue develops between the academic and professional cultures. Anastas (2010) points out that while social work is a profession, being a professor is a profession as well. They are two separate professions with different missions and credentials, but similar ideals. They share the commitment of service to others, competence, ethical conduct, and dedication to work. However, Seidl (2000) suggests that few practice faculty would have their own published work in their course bibliographies. This he claims to be a measure of scholarly commitment, and he proposes that more value has been placed on professionalism than on scholarship. Anastas (2010) concurs when she says of the social work profession "its practice—the application of concepts to interventions in the real world—is a focus of its research…" (p. 193). She contends that not enough is published. Although each claims to maintain a respect for the other, it is as if practitioners don't value research as relevant and researchers don't value clinical judgment.

In her 2007 Message from the President of the New York City Chapter of NASW, Rose Starr wrote, "Practice is our purpose… (the) profession's survival requires that we not lose our essential value to those we serve." Kemp (1998) underscores that practice informs teaching and practice experience is essential to a credible professional education. Experience contributes to the education of a competent student by connecting the practicum to classroom learning. It allows for the provision of examples and conveys meaning to academic experience. But, Videka-Sherman (1998) responds that requiring practice experience for teaching faculty does not ensure practice, scholarship, or teaching competence. She refers to the 2-year practice requirement as a "vestige of the apprenticeship model of professional education" (p. 341).

CSWE asserts another outside influence on the deterioration in the value of practice experience in teaching. Although the requirement never applied to elective courses, CSWE has always maintained requirements for teaching required practice courses. In 1994, an MSW from an accredited program and two or more years of post-master's experience in professional social work experience were required (Thyer, 2000). In 2001, this was changed to say that an MSW in a CSWE accredited program was needed and at least 2 years postbaccalaureate or post-master's social work degree practice experience (CSWE, 2001). Again, the standard was reduced in the 2008 revision of the CSWE EPAS. The current version states that to teach required practice courses, a master's degree in social work is required from a CSWE accredited program and at least 2 years of social work practice experience. It is significant that the word "professional" has been removed, and only pre-degree experience is required. This presents the interesting paradox that students could experience faculty who are legally unable to practice or supervise that in which students will want to practice and become licensed.

In economic hard times, these reduced standards underscore the use of more adjunct or contingent faculty. According to the American Association of University Professors between 1976 and 2005, the use of adjuncts grew by 200 %, while tenure-track faculty positions increased by only 17 %. Many schools are now hiring a separate, non-tenure-track faculty to teach clinical courses. These contingent positions receive less pay than the tenured or tenure-track faculty, therefore costing the university less money. The adjuncts also provide a relief in that they allow the rest of the faculty time to research and write for publication. And, practice takes a backseat once more as the part-time faculty have no representation in the governance process. There is no voice for the practice faculty in curricula matters, hiring practices, or tenure and promotion decisions (Johnson & Munch, 2010).

While job applicants with both practice experience and degree credentials are preferred, the momentum is shifting from the MSW to requiring the PhD for tenure-track faculty positions. Not only does hiring assistant professors with doctoral credentials legitimize the profession as an academic endeavor but also it promotes the concept of the scientist-practitioner. Emphasis is placed on practice informed by research findings and the generation of evidence-based interventions for vulnerable populations. Research becomes the valued tool for determining the effectiveness of practice. In the teaching of practice knowledge and skills, evidence-based interventions and the broader research base become the scholarship that is seen to enrich education and curriculum development. It is the scholar, not the practitioner, leading the progress in practice theory (Johnson & Munch, 2010).

An unintended but welcome by-product of the pressure for publication is that there is a growing interdisciplinary community. The need to use journals from other disciplines has promoted access to new learning. Some schools of social work are hiring faculty with doctorates and no social work qualification, which reflects an exciting interdisciplinary potential (Johnson & Munch, 2010).

Conclusion

Passion in politics, economic demands, and the influence of professional associations create the perfect storm. Schools of social work are in the throes of an ever-changing environment, full of polarized emotions and changing belief systems. Perhaps it is still possible to renew the value and place of practice experience in education. There is much to be gained and much that is lost as education in social work struggles to survive, to grow, and to gain in status and respect.

References

Anastas, J. W. (2010). *Teaching in social work: An educator's guide to theory and practice*. New York, NY: Columbia University Press.

Council on Social Work Education. (2001). *Educational policy and accreditation standards*. Alexandria, VA: Author. http://www.cswe.org/Accreditation/Reaffirmation-2001EPAS.aspx

Council on Social Work Education. (2007). *Statement from the Council on Social Work Education, CSWE in the news: Social justice and accreditation*. CSWE Office of the Executive Director. Alexandria, VA: Council on Social Work Education.

Council on Social Work Education. (2008). *Educational policy and accreditation standards*. Alexandria, VA: Author. http://www.cswe.org/Accreditation/Reaffirmation.aspx.

Hartman, A. (1991). Words create worlds. *Social Work, 36*(4), 275–276.

Hyde, C. A., & Ruth, B. J. (2002). Multicultural content and class participation: Do students self censor? *Journal of Social Work Education, 38*(2), 241–256.

Johnson, Y., & Munch, S. (2010). Faculty with practice experience: The new dinosaurs in the social work academy. *Journal of Social Work Education, 46*(1), 57–66.

Kemp, S. P. (1998). Should two years of practice experience be essential to teach required practice classes? Yes! *Journal of Social Work Education, 34*(3), 329–334.

Longres, J. F. (1994). Bias, devaluation, and stereotyping. *Journal of Social Work Education, 30*(3), 284–285.

Magna Publications. (2004). Student academic freedom debate hits campuses, too. *Magna Student Affairs Leader, National On Campus Report 32*(12). http://www.magnapubs.com/issues/magnapubs_nocr/32_12/

National Association of Scholars. (2007). The scandal of social work education. http://www.nas.org/polArticles.cfm?doc_id=26

National Association of Social Work. (1999). *Code of ethics*. Washington, DC: Author.

Pelton, L. (2001). Social justice and social work. *Journal of Social Work Education, 37*(3), 433–439.

Shiell, T. C. (2006). Three conceptions of academic freedom. In E. Gerstmann & M. J. Streb (Eds.), *Academic freedom at the dawn of a new century: How terrorism, governments & culture wars impact free speech* (pp. 17–40). Stanford, CA: Stanford University Press.

Seidl, F. (2000). Should licensure be required for faculty who teach direct practice courses? No! *Journal of Social Work Education, 36*(2), 193–196.

Simpson, G. A., Williams, J. C., & Segall, A. B. (2007). Social work education and clinical learning. *Clinical Social Work Journal, 35*(1), 3–14.

Stoesz, D. (2008). Social work agonistes. *Academic Questions, 21*(2), 164–182.

Streb, M. J. (2006). The reemergence of the academic freedom debate. In E. Gerstmann & M. J. Streb (Eds.), *Academic freedom at the dawn of a new century: How terrorism, governments & culture wars impact free speech* (pp. 3–16). Stanford, CA: Stanford University Press.

Thyer, B. A. (2000). Should licensure be required for faculty who teach direct practice courses? Yes! *Journal of Social Work Education, 36*(2), 187–201.

Uelman, G. (1992). The price of free speech: Campus hate speech codes. *Santa Clara University, Issues in Ethics 5*(2). http://www.scu.edu/ethics/publications/iie/v5n2/codes.html

USA PATRIOT Act of 2001, P.L. 105-107 (2001); H.R. 107-236, pt.1 at 42 (2001).

Videka-Sherman, L. (1998). Should two years of practice experience be essential to teach required practice classes? No! *Journal of Social Work Education, 34*(3), 337–341.

Will, G. (2007, October 14). Code of coercion. *Washington Post*, p. B7.

Chapter 8
Silence in the Clinical Hour: A Time to Speak

Billie Lee Violette

The purpose of this chapter is to bring psychoanalytic practice (in-depth clinical work) closer to the consideration of war and environmental factors that add stress to all our lives both inside and outside of the consulting room. Living in the context of two US wars abroad and a cultural war within the country, I believed I was able to put this out of my mind while working. I now think this was a fantasy. To elaborate on this, I will start with accounts of analysts operating in the context of World War II. Then I will describe my experience with three Jewish patients at the time of the Israeli–Lebanese war of 2006. Stepping aside and looking at how our psychoanalytic focus on the individual contributes to our apparent insularity from cultural problems, including war, I want to look at our discipline from two points of view: how we as professionals are related to the culture at large and how we view "the frame" (the structure and principles we use to provide safety) in our consulting rooms.

Psychoanalysis in WWII

During WWII and the bombing of London, there was a side war going on within the British Psychoanalytic Society. Anna Freud and Melanie Klein disagreed over the internal world of young children and whether or not they could be analyzed. Anna Freud thought children needed an educative and supportive approach in treatment, taking the position that prior to the Oedipus complex (between 3 and 5 years of age) the child's psyche was not consolidated enough for analysis. Klein disagreed and elucidated a rich internal life of part object relations prior to the traditional Oedipus complex. This disagreement resulted in the famous "controversial discussions."

B.L. Violette (✉)
National Study Group, AAPCSW, Psychoanalytic Institute of Northern California, San Francisco, CA 94118, USA
e-mail: billieviolette@yahoo.com

E. Ruderman and C. Tosone (eds.), *Contemporary Clinical Practice: The Holding Environment Under Assault*, Essential Clinical Social Work Series,
DOI 10.1007/978-1-4614-4124-3_8, © Springer Science+Business Media New York 2013

However, it was James Strachey's perception that behind the theoretical disagreements there was a fight for power and control of the British Psychoanalytic Society; and thus, candidates to teach and analyze were pressured to line up behind one or the other. This preoccupation with the conflict between the two women leds John Rickman to become outraged at the British analysts' insensitivity and disregard for the public (Grosskurth, 1986).

Grosskurth (1986) describes a British Psychoanalytic Society meeting during the bombing of London, in which the analysts were discussing hatred and aggression when:

> ...an air raid started. However, the members were so absorbed in their own battle that they remained glued to their seats. Winnicott drew their attention to the uproar outdoors: "I should like to point out that there is an air raid going on," [and the meeting continued.] At the next meeting the chairman felt it was expedient to decide what action should be taken if another air raid occurred during the meeting. It was agreed that the meeting should be stopped temporarily to allow members who had responsibilities at home to leave, and the others should carry their chairs to the basement to continue the discussion. In fact there was no decrease in the numbers attending the meeting until much later. (p. 321)

During this same period of time, Melanie Klein left London for the countryside, where she analyzed 10-year-old Richard whose father had gone off to the war. Richard drew warplanes and submarines. Klein, who felt it was her task to analyze psychic reality, explained to him that his bumping ships together represented his parent's sexual intercourse (Grosskurth, 1986). This may seem incomprehensible to us today, but my own recent experiences allow me to better understand the avoidance of a reality you are helpless to control.

To focus on the battles in London is to give an incomplete picture or a one-sided picture of the situation. While still living in Vienna, Anna Freud, who was originally trained as a teacher for small children before becoming a psychoanalyst, was taken to Nazi headquarters for questioning because she was a Jew, a situation she reportedly handled with aplomb (Young-Bruehl, 1988). She and her father only reluctantly left Austria, where they eventually lost family members to the Holocaust. After relocating in England, Anna Freud remained in London with her father during the bombing and established shelters for children and adolescents. She and her colleagues took copious notes on the children's adjustment and involved the parents as much as was possible.

This model of research is instrumental in teaching us how children deal with stress and separations. Robertson's (a social worker) study of the emotional trauma on children, separated from their mother during hospitalization, is an outgrowth of Anna Freud's work. Bowlby's work on attachment and Spitz's work on children in infant nurseries are other examples, where British psychoanalytic knowledge was used to study the effects of separation of the baby from the mother, "the person in the environment" rather than the consulting room only (Young-Bruehl, 1988). This research on the individual child in the situation has had lasting impact up to the present time. Today we keep the parents connected to the child in hospital situations. Qualitative and quantitative research combined with Anna Freud's direct community service cannot be overlooked when attempting to integrate psychoanalytic theory with other disciplines and the culture at large. The reluctance to study the "the person in the environment" has allowed analysts to focus on the individual in the context of the consulting room only. This same reluctance seems to be a facet of many disciplines to struggle with the complexities of human experience—for each field of endeavor attempts to delimit itself to a paradigm that is conceived of as manageable for study.

Recent War Experience

During July and August of 2006, the time of the Israeli/Lebanese war, I was working with three Jewish women whose family backgrounds included war and dislocation. All three turned out to have narcissistic difficulties, which I attribute not simply to their faulty mothering but also to the trauma their families experienced—not only carried through conscious narrative but unconsciously manifested through their affect and behavior (acting out).

Anna, American born and raised, was originally a small business owner but obtained an advanced degree and went into administration and program development to establish services for veterans. She was the stepdaughter of a woman who was taken out of Germany on the kinder train at the age of 13. The stepmother was alternately warm, and then very physically and emotionally abusive. The father ignored what was happening in the family, no doubt probably very relieved to have help with his children following the suicide of Anna's mother. Thus, violence in the past was recreated in the familial home. Fearing that loss of control would put her in danger, this patient managed me on a very distant rein, regaling me with tales of her accomplishments, until such time that circumstances caused her to collapse and become fragmented. Anna has been able to work with me over considerable time, and following her breakdown, has been able to recognize that I have a subjectivity of my own, and has integrated me into her psyche as a comforting object. In other words, she feels safe enough to think.

Beth, raised and educated near Tel Aviv, was the granddaughter of German Jews dislocated into Israel prior to WWII, and her grandmother later lost a son in one of the Israeli wars. The grandmother never recovered from this loss. She was the primary caretaker during the week for the patient. The grandmother psychically confused the patient with her lost child, creating for Beth an internal world of identity confusion and violence. Following a career in science, the patient went to medical school and obtained a psychiatry residency in the San Francisco Bay Area. She was particularly sensitive to patients whose earliest traumas created severe disorders of the self. With me, she was an entitled princess and I was a nanny not deserving of a professional fee. Despite my lack of compliance with my assigned role, she continued to use me for a sense of stability and consistency. After much deliberation, Beth returned to Israel because of family pressure, the benefits of being with her wealthy family, and because she longed for her mother to make up for abandoning her to her grandmother.

Carol, Israeli born, was from another displaced German family that was highly dysfunctional in every way. The parents saw their children as creatures to provide academic status and financial security for them. Carol became a mathematician but lacked meaning in her life; she became very identified with the Palestinian cause and became a community organizer on their behalf. Then she got a green card to study women's issues at the University of California. In the therapy she had a severe diffusion of identity and presented herself as both male and masterful, and at the same time extremely afraid that I would not recognize her for whom she was. When Carol's academic green card expired, although she had a choice to renew it, she returned to Israel to do community organization.

In summary, all three tried to work in disparate fields but fell back into helper-rescuer roles. Their own basic emotional needs were taken over by the traumatized needs of their families. In the transference with me, I had little subjectivity.

As Beth and Carol were returning to Israel at the time of the war with Lebanon, I noted, much to my consternation, that they never mentioned any anxiety. Thus, I expressed my concern. They seemed totally untroubled by their choices, informing me that it was not a problem, as they knew how to stay safe. As I was raising questions about their returning, it was completely out of my conscious awareness that my own country, the USA, was involved in the Israel/Palestinian problem and that we were in two other wars in the Middle East (Iraq and Afghanistan). They, however, challenged me on my lack of awareness. They pointed out the danger in living in the USA, referring to 9/11, quoting statistics about the crime and gun rate in our country, and they noted that I lived near areas of high urban crime. It became clear that to exist in these circumstances, one uses denial.

Going back to the American, much identified with her Jewish heritage, Anna was very disturbed by these wars. It was during this same period that she recalled that prominent actor had been picked up by the police for drunk driving and was quoted, during his arrest, as saying the Jews were the cause of our wars. She talked of being very frightened about a backlash against the Jews in the USA. What I noted was that the American-Jewish patient expressed her fright. It was palatable and I likewise felt very frightened and almost paranoid.

To summarize, the two Israelis denied their fear, and my bringing up the piece about their external reality led them to make me the frightened one, while they remained powerful and in control. The American patient, existing in a relatively safer environment, was able to talk about her fear, and I felt my own as I tried to integrate her experience into my own psyche to understand her anxiety. Following these experiences, I presented my ideas for this chapter to some colleagues in a psychoanalytic writing group. Here are some responses:

(a) "If I was in a bomb shelter and my country was being bombed, I'd probably do the same thing"—as the British analysts.
(b) "The night of the Battle at Amiens, Bion and his troops read poetry. That was the best that could be done for the next day they were all killed except for Bion."

There was little interest in my topic and the group moved on to the subject of writing. Only one person, a psychiatrist who was not an analyst, came to me afterwards to say she thought my topic was important. Was I experiencing in current time what I described during British Psychoanalytic Society meetings of WWII, a way of going on which left me to deal with helplessness? Was lack of interest in my paper representing an which left attitude toward the world at large? Have we become so specialized as analysts that topics beyond technique and theory are of little interest?

Contextualizing Our Discipline

In *Constructing the Self, Constructing America* (1995), Cushman puts forth the idea that our theories replicate cultural paradigms—psychoanalytic ideas about being a "container" and the focus on "the self" are two. In American history, violence against others seen as less than human is part of our cultural heritage; two prime examples are the killing of the indigenous people to establish the country and the capturing of Africans for use as slaves. Cushman (1995) asserts that Americans are able to romanticize this past and have gone on to see themselves as self-made, self-contained persons—a useful perception of the self in establishing the frontier, in which separation from extended family and friends was the norm. With the onset of industrialization, there was a further break down in family and communal identity. Cushman (1995) suggests the container of the self is a very useful construct for US capitalism and materialism: we have become consumers buying products to enhance our power and desirability, and to fill up our empty interior, while fueling the wheels of capitalism and its deregulation. By focusing on the intrapsychic versus the interpersonal, Cushman (1995) concludes that we as analysts buy into the current culture unwittingly, by purporting to provide something to help fill up the empty person. Furthermore, we are compliasant with society's breakdown by perpetuating the conception of the person as a self-contained bounded individual.

Cushman (1995) laments psychoanalysts' theorizing about the patient's past (in the nuclear family) and the faulting of parents for pathology. He cites particularly Klein for her relentless focus on the phantasy, Kohut for mother blaming, and American ego psychology for promoting adaption to the culture that supports patriarchy. He posits that by doing this, we ignore the social realities of current day life contributing to our patient's difficulties.

By way of contrast, Cushman (1995) proposes that the work of Henry Stack Sullivan and Merton Gill focuses on the "here and now" and how the patient interacts in the present with the therapist as well as those outside the consulting room. He critiques ideas that have been integrated into general psychoanalytic theory as relentless analysis of the "there and then" and as such, less useful. Relational psychoanalytic theory, as well as advancements in the other theoretical schools, is trying to deal with the dilemma of the isolated one-person mind by the two-person paradigm. I think Cushman would suggest, however, that the relationalists do not go far enough to include another or third dimension—awareness of the cultural surround—so as to wake up ourselves, and thus our patients, to the cultural surround and our role as citizens (versus consumers).

Naomi Klein (2007), writing on politics and economics, coined the term "disaster capitalism." She asserts that by promulgating the belief that everyone is independent, rational, and deserving of a gun (a rugged individual) and the anti-regulation economic theories of Milton Freidman, the neoconservatives in the USA have devised a strategy in which natural and man-made disasters (Hurricane Katrina and the war in Iraq are two) are used to colonize more resources for the powerful. When the population of a disaster area is too traumatized by the shock to think rationally, the strategy is to keep the population confused so that certain factions of American capitalists can step in with their own agenda. Klein (2007) quotes Freidman as describing Katrina as an opportunity to permanently reform the public school system into a voucher system that could be spent at private institutions, run for a profit, and subsidized by the state.

Studying how war and capitalism influences our unconscious seems an important step in this direction. Considering Cushman's (1995) critique on theory, the dilemma for the individual therapist is how to keep safety in the analytic frame and promote the transference. Then the question we can ask ourselves: what do we represent to the patient when war and current culture seep into our pre- and subconscious minds? Do the accoutrements of our offices and our lifestyle represent democratic philosophy of social justice or that of success and consumerism?

Adam Curtis (2002) explored the evolution of self-orientation in a documentary *The Century of the Self*, which describes how American capitalism has used psychoanalytic knowledge to promote political agendas abroad and at home so as to manufacture a perceived need for material goods. Mrs. Sigmund Freud's nephew, Edward Bernays, became the father of public relations, which Curtis (2002) presents as synonymous with propaganda. Bernays translated Freud's work on unconscious motivation for application in industry and the development of consumerism. His ideas were used in Germany by Hitler to stir up the masses against the Jews. Curtis (2002) presents examples in the film in which women are encouraged to take up smoking and men to buy new cars as symbols of penis strength and power. Mental health professionals bought into the opportunity industry by working in these environments without considering how our materialistic trend has included the loss of identity as a citizen and the importance of community concerns.

It is only recently that psychoanalysis has taken up citizenship as an important aspect of the self. Lear (2000) has connected Aristotle's Nicomachean Ethics to psychoanalysis in his book, *Happiness, Death, and the Remainder of Life*. Following up on Socrates' discussions with his followers, Aristotle wrote on the subject of happiness. These early philosophers conceived of happiness as leading a civilized existence—being a better citizen. This is not only an ethical stance but a teleological one as well. It provides the person a goal or ideal for which to strive and which connects him/her to the world outside.

Lear's (2000) discussion of this is complicated for he describes the infant's experience and affect as contained by language and the culture with an "excess" or a "remainder" of energy and experience that is not contained. Aristotle, he proposes, gives this remainder a place or goal in his concept of citizenship. Lear explains that in lieu of citizenship, Freud (who lived through two world wars, I would add) gave us the death drive in which aggression becomes conceived of as energy moving backwards, a non-teleological stance. Lear argues that what to do with the excess is culturally determined and that psychoanalysis contributes to this process by freeing up the mind for creative thought. Considering the threat to civilized existence and the survival of the planet and if we believe in the inherent worth of each individual and democracy as the highest form of government, then returning to Aristotle's value system of being a citizen and using our minds is vital.

Samuels addresses analysts' avoidance of political reality in *The Political Psyche* (1993). He (Samuels, 2009) has studied psychoanalysts' failure to analyze their own and their patients' attitudes toward money as well. Thus, not only do analysts fail to understand whole parts of ourselves, we may not be doing our job as citizens of a democracy, inadvertently participating in promoting consumers, not citizens. Unwillingly supporting a more insulated life, we perpetuate our capitalistic society in which wealth is gained from catastrophes and wars.

There are many reasons we can identify psychoanalysis' isolation from the larger culture. After psychoanalysis was introduced in the USA, psychiatrists obtained a monopoly on the profession, thus excluding other professionals. The prestige of psychiatrists and the fees they could charge made psychoanalysis accessible for the more advantaged, both for those who practiced it and those with the resources of time and money to receive it. The influence and prestige of European analysts who immigrated to the USA during WWII also contributed to a distancing of psychoanalysis from cultural issues. Originally more politically oriented in their outlook, the trauma of the war led these analysts to retreat into a more isolated view of the analytic subject as a defense (Jacoby, 1975).

Thus, an American version of classical psychoanalysis developed which focused on ego development and analysis of defense, eschewing input from psychoanalysis in other countries. Further adding to an insularity was the fact that after completing medical school, psychoanalytic training was done outside of universities in institutes of the American Psychoanalytic Association, an elite system whose political agenda consisted in perpetuating the status quo (Jacoby, 1975; Kirsner, 2000). This hegemony remained unchallenged until the 1980s when psychologists successfully challenged the psychiatric monopoly that constrained who could be trained in institutes. Psychologists were instrumental in developing the relational school of psychoanalysis, which integrated theory from different schools of thought hitherto divorced from ego psychology, e.g., Sullivan, Klein, the British Middle School, and so forth (Greenberg & Mitchell 1983; Horowitz 1987). This, however, has not made for more accessibility of psychoanalysis into the culture at large. In my experience, those trained tend to be the more intellectual and privileged, and not politically or systems oriented. And in the 1980s, I found that the changes in the US insurance industry limited mental health care and further marginalized psychoanalytic thought and practice in favor of medications and behavioral and cognitive therapies.

Writing on lack of diversity in institutes, Eisold (1994) has discussed the stress of the work itself, the introversion of analysts, as well as the lack of connection to the outside world and an elitist attitude toward other disciplines. A major part of an analyst's time is devoted to relating in pairs (supervision and analysis); thus, the focus remains on the individual rather than the individual in the larger group. The lack of diversity with which Eisold was concerned was that of the curriculum, not that the trainees were primarily middle- and upper middle-class Caucasians.

Container for the Self

Moving from the macro of our professions' relationship to culture into the micro of how we operate, I want to return to psychoanalytic practice and the frame of the treatment hour. Our rigid adherence to theory can impede our meeting the patient where the patient is, and at the same time our psychoanalytic acumen can help us know when the patient needs a tight frame excluding the outside world. Our own stresses and unresolved issues play a role in our ability to reflect on what the patient needs. Here are some questions to ask.

Regarding theory per se, do we view our real selves in the analytic hour to be an aspect of what the patient uses to promote new models of experience, or do we see growth as coming primarily from interpretation of the transference? And then do our theoretical preferences prejudice us to deal with only certain material that is presented, and thus exclude other material? I see the Kleinian notion of always looking for and finding evidence for the weekend breaks a classic example of this.

Regarding the person of the analyst, do we feel a need to bring in external reality like I may have done in my earlier examples? Or do we avoid external reality to feel in control? How do we represent ourselves with our social/cultural anxieties when those the patient brings up are similar to our own?

Recently, Joy, a patient with psychotic depression and anxiety as well as dissociative states, asked me about the 2008 US presidential election and for whom I was going to vote. I hedged and asked her about her thoughts. I got a picture of her thinking. However, I think she may have been asking for guidance, and it perhaps would have served her to tell her I was voting for Barack Obama and why. I regretted having hedged, but a couple of weeks later, she brought up the subject again. This time I told her I was voting for Obama and elaborated upon why. Then I learned was that she was leaning that direction, but would be going counter to her family and many members in her conservative Christian church.

Here are some questions that are relevant to the person of the patient. Does the patient have a coherent structure? Are the social anxieties social anxieties per se or are they manifestations of defective ego boundaries needing shoring up by a tight container or frame? Are the social anxieties an externalization or projection of internal conflicts?

What about that which is not brought up in the treatment? Something can be quite relevant by its absence and then the question comes up whether it is denial, repression, developmental lack, or an avoidance; or is it a belief that the patient does not think it is relevant for analysis and/or has other some reason to hide this concern?

Are the social conditions coming into the analysis environmental stress only or environmental stress triggering earlier trauma or both? These are certainly questions we can raise about Klein's therapy with Richard.

Do our institutes and analytic groups hold us holding our patients, and how do they do that? Would we be viewed as less than analytic to bring up the stressful cultural reality?

Returning to Joy, the woman who asked me for whom I was voting, provides an illustration of the complexity in which these questions have to be dealt. Joy had an apocalyptic childhood. She was born premature and cared for in a neonatal nursery, and the mother returned home to another suburb and left the baby's total care to the nursing staff. Joy's parents divorced, and because of financial strains on the mother, the family moved frequently, resulting in Joy changing schools multiple times. As a result Joy had major problems in coping with school and lacked a stable friendship group. The mother's response to Joy's anxiety was to let her go into a safe place: a closet with a blanket, reminiscent of a uterine existence. Because of the family instability, the mother remarried a very "strong" man with a reliable job who turned out to have a violent/sadistic side; Joy repeatedly attempted to intervene in physical battles between the parents. The mother died suddenly when Joy was 8 years of age, and she went to live with her biological father and a troubled rageful stepmother. There, she was repeatedly molested by a neighbor. As an adolescent, she ran away and was rescued by a Fundamentalist Christian family. She eventually married the Christian family's son after graduating from a Christian college. She then did missionary work in different African countries until she lost her faith and had a breakdown precipitated by a minister's sexual overtures toward her.

This patient's psyche is filled with death and violence (repetitive dreams of dead people). The gun collection that she owned (given to her by her stepfather) had to be locked away after she shot at squirrels in the backyard and threatened to shoot herself. For the first couple of years of treatment (four times a week with day treatment and medication backup), the patient regularly cut her arms to get tension out of her body.

I learned that in the place of parental introjection of self-care, Joy internalized a Christian Fundamentalist idea of Jesus first, others next, and yourself last. She actually believed that it was good to suffer like Jesus. Her internal object world consisted of a rageful punitive superego and a guilty bad self. She could only do good acts but not get the good inside her, thus developing adhesive relationships with parental figures having internalized a frantic distressed mother who could not keep Joy's emotional needs in mind. Separation from me, her analyst, resulted in a painful sensation of part of herself being ripped away. This was followed by an ongoing empty loneliness, and finally rage.

This case calls for a tight frame for Joy is extremely depressed and has defects in her ability to self-sooth. Her concrete adherence to following rules from various parts of the Bible made it clear that she could not think in regard to regulating herself and standing up to others. She used denial, splitting, and dissociation as defenses. She has trouble leaving the sessions and was not able to respond to my interpretations regarding this; I eventually extended her session to 1 1/2 h, which helped her to manage her anxiety so she could leave more contained. In the sessions, there would be an ongoing silence in which she felt depleted and wanted something from me to keep on going. The silence seemed to represent an absent mother, a void she could not tolerate. I could sometimes find small bodily clues that gave a window into feelings for which she did not have words.

In Joy's case, I would not introduce political/social issues (that no doubt did affect her) as I wanted to contain the early traumatized parts of her. However, when she asked about for whom I was voting, it was clear that the political scene was in her mind, and the second time she asked, I felt she needed something "real" or she would not have asked again. Not wanting to seem like an oracle, I wanted to reason out loud for her why I was making my particular choice. This of course revealed my own anxieties about the political situation, but we were in it together.

Conclusion

I have been tacking back and forth between in-depth clinical work and the sociopolitical surround in which we operate in a time of war. To come full circle, let me further elaborate on how cultural issues have been affected in my work. First, let me think again about my three Jewish patients. Contextualizing myself as an American clinician, let me expose my lack of sensitivity. The need to be in constant contact with the family was anathema to me and may have prejudiced me against the significance of returning to Israel where being with family and friends was as important as protecting one's self. Then having never been attacked for my ethnicity in any major way (until 9/11), I have a different sense of vulnerability and may not have processed the unconscious guilt at abandoning their parents and grandparents, survivors of the Holocaust. Being the granddaughter of homesteaders in the American West, Anglo-Saxon Protestants, and growing up on "Westerns" in books, movies, and television, I had unwittingly romanticized the individualism that Cushman (1995) writes about. I received social work training prior to becoming an analyst, in which the influence of the environment was addressed (although I slipped through without understanding much of my own cultural embeddedness), which enabled me to introduce the impact of the cultural/societal situation into the consulting room without much guilt about whether I was analytic enough. Whether this was in the best interest of the Israeli patients is questionable. Did I interfere with the need for the patient to have a secure holding environment? Psychoanalytic understanding can be of help here.

On the other hand, none of the psychoanalytic study groups in which I have participated focus on our own vulnerabilities, our cultural predilections, our prejudices, politics, or our beliefs. These issues come up more incidentally. It is clear that we have to be able to split ourselves into the clinical role to operate in the hour. But we need to build a place in psychoanalytic training to reflect on our cultural embeddedness so that we might be able to find some ways to connect the psychoanalytic understanding of the person (awareness of the unconscious) to the ethical questions of being a person in the larger world.

References

Curtis, A. (Producer & Director) (2002). *The century of the self.* London, England: British Broadcasting Corporation.
Cushman, P. (1995). *Constructing the self, constructing America.* Menlo Park, CA: Addison-Wesley.
Eisold, K. (1994). The intolerance of diversity in psychoanalytic institutes. *International Journal of Psychoanalysis, 75*, 785–800.
Greenberg, J. R., & Mitchell, S. A. (1983). *Object relations in psychoanalytic theory.* Cambridge, MA: Harvard University Press.
Grosskurth, P. (1986). *Melanie Klein: Her world and her work.* New York, NY: Alfred A. Knopf.
Horowitz, J. (1987). History of the Psychoanalytic Institute of Northern California. (Unpublished document).
Jacoby, R. (1975). *A critique of contemporary psychology from Adler to Laing.* Boston, MA: Beacon.
Kirsner, D. (2000). *Unfree associations: Inside psychoanalytic institutes.* London, England: Process Press.
Klein, N. (2007). *The shock doctrine: The rise of disaster capitalism.* New York, NY: Picador.
Lear, J. (2000). *Happiness, death, and the remainder of life.* Cambridge, MA: Harvard University Press.
Samuels, A. (1993). *The political psyche.* New York, NY: Routledge.
Samuels, A. (2009, May). *The political subject of analysis: The impact of social 'shock and awe'.* Paper presented at the Psychoanalytic Institute of Northern California conference, *The renaissance of western politics: The good-enough leader, relational economics, and an empathic foreign policy*, Berkeley, CA. http://pincsf.org/events/papers/A-Samuels_Paper_5_30_09_1.pdf.
Young-Bruehl, E. (1988). *Anna Freud.* New York, NY: W.W. Norton.

Chapter 9
Real Experiences Revisited: The Significance of Attachment, Separation, and Loss in Adult Psychotherapy

Pat Sable

Once considered outside the realm of psychoanalytic theory and treatment, clinical observations as well as research on the trauma of conditions such as family violence, child abuse, and neglect have shown that real experiences have a substantial influence on a person's development and functioning throughout the life cycle. In fact, acknowledgement of the impact of actual events on emotional and physical well-being is now so prevalent in psychological thinking that Goldstein (2009) recently wrote "psychoanalytic theories have expanded to encompass…the impact of interpersonal, social and cultural factors on personality functioning" (p. 10).

One theory that has contributed to this "widening scope of psychoanalysis" (Stone, 1954) is attachment theory, founded by the British psychoanalyst, John Bowlby, who had the conviction that "the real world of human relationships" (Schwartz, 2008), together with the surrounding environment, was central to clinical understanding and the process of psychotherapy. His work is part of the paradigm shift that has seen psychoanalysis move from drive theory toward a relational perspective, a perspective that began with Fairbairn's concept that we are basically object seeking rather than pleasure seeking (Reeves, 2008; Schwartz, 2007). Bowlby (1969, 1973, 1980), moreover, suggested replacing drive theory with an ethological-evolutionary framework in order to explain that there is an innate tendency, evidenced in both young children and animals, to seek out and sustain proximity to attachment figures for the biological function of protection and security.

Although Bowlby (1973) became known for his innovative conceptualization of the mother–child bond, he saw the need for secure attachment to exist throughout life. He further emphasized that security was related to having a "steady relationship" with a "familiar environment" which he called the "outer ring of life-maintaining systems" and which he saw as complementary to a person's "inner ring of systems that maintain physiological homeostasis" (p. 150). Because some of Bowlby's

P. Sable (✉)
National Study Group, AAPCSW, USC School of Social Work,
Los Angeles, CA 90049, USA
e-mail: sable@usc.edu

E. Ruderman and C. Tosone (eds.), *Contemporary Clinical Practice: The Holding Environment Under Assault*, Essential Clinical Social Work Series,
DOI 10.1007/978-1-4614-4124-3_9,

concepts have become so familiar and popular, it can be difficult to remember and appreciate how bold and controversial this addition to psychoanalytic thinking was at the time. But Bowlby's approach, which included his call for theory to be based on research, has been substantiated, modified, and expanded by findings from attachment-based research, neuroscience, and animal studies. As Fonagy said in a recent interview (White & Schwartz, 2007), "psychoanalysis plus attachment theory is fantastic" (p. 60); it is an injection into psychoanalysis that allows therapists to relate to clients in more open and flexible ways.

I have found that attachment theory offers an approach to therapy that incorporates both internal and interpersonal dimensions of a client's situation without giving priority to one over the other. Developed out of ethology (the observation of animal behavior) and psychoanalysis, it is compatible with the social work person-in-environmental tradition. The link Bowlby (1979) made between experiences in the real world and vulnerability to psychological disturbance reflects a social work stance, and he credits his association with several social workers early in his career with influencing some of the ideas that he was formulating. Even late in his career while speaking to a social work group in London, he said that he "owed (social workers) a great deal of debt, gratitude," that he "learned everything from social workers" such as their focus on "actual experiences" over fantasy (Sable, 2010).

This chapter explores the therapeutic implications of this fundamental tenet of attachment theory, that of the lifelong significance of real experiences on a person's emotional and physical well-being. In particular, there is a focus on aspects of the theory that are relevant to adult psychotherapy. For example, two concepts that therapists have found helpful, secure base and attachment patterns, can only be understood within the context of actual experiences. Yet, because psychoanalysis was traditionally intrapsychic, "attachment-related psychodynamics" have not been as spelled out (Eagle & Wolitzky, 2009; Mikulincer & Shaver, 2007).

It is proposed that attachment concepts change our understanding of development which in turn gives us a new way of thinking about our clients' distress and how we carry out treatment. It is further proposed that, as we are teaching in MSW programs, it is essential to pay attention to the various systems that can be having an impact on a client's distress. This effort does not take away from our concern about our clients' inner thoughts and feelings. It does have a bearing on how we listen and respond during a session.

In paving the way to integrate the reality of real experiences into psychoanalysis, Bowlby (1973) used results from research on disrupted or broken attachments to point out the damage that these kinds of experiences could have on a person's relational functioning. Discussion is organized around the three concepts of attachment, separation, and loss that illustrate his position and are the ones that made him famous. They are represented in the titles of his trilogy *Attachment* (1969), *Separation* (1973), and *Loss* (1980) and provide the foundation of his theory. Each of these three sections also addresses the contemporary versions of this "psychobiological mind-and-body theory" (Kraemer et al., 2005) as it has been updated by neuroscience and attachment-based studies such as begun by Ainsworth et al. (1978) and later expanded by scores of attachment researchers. I begin with an overview of the theory and then consider how the concepts of separation and loss introduce a theoretical understanding of real experiences as well as guidelines for an attachment-based psychoanalytic therapy.

Attachment

I first met John Bowlby in Canada in 1978 where he was the featured speaker at a conference titled "Current Issues in Child Psychiatry," sponsored by the Clarke Institute of Psychiatry. The focus on child issues reflected the prominence Dr. Bowlby had achieved for his insight on the importance of a child's early experiences with caregivers. In formulating what is now recognized and accepted as a "lifespan developmental theory" (Crowell, Fraley, & Shaver, 1999) as well as a theory of affect regulation (Schore, 1994; Sroufe & Waters, 1977), Bowlby (1969, 1973, 1980) combined his training in psychoanalytic object relations theories with concepts from ethology, evolution theory, cognitive psychology, and control theory. He applied concepts from information processing to explain defenses which he called defensive exclusion.

An ethological account of attachment starts with the premise that infants need available and responsive caregivers who they can learn to count on for protection from threat or danger. Bowlby (1969) introduced the notion of an attachment behavioral system (a concept he borrowed from ethology) to explain that infants are equipped with a number of instinctive behaviors such as crying or clinging that signal the need for proximity and support, thus increasing the likelihood of their survival and eventual reproductive success. The attachment system is conceptualized as an innate regulatory system, geared to contend with circumstances related to security, but how it becomes organized and manifest in later relationships depends on experiences with others (Fonagy, 2001; Shaver & Mikulincer, 2007).

Schore (1994, 1997, 2003a, b) has supported Bowlby's contention about real experiences with findings from developmental neuroscience while also expanding the theory with evidence that a caregiver not only shields the baby from environmental threats but also helps regulate both positive and negative feelings. Furthermore, Schore (1999) and Siegel (1999) have documented how early attachment experiences are processed and stored in implicit memory in the limbic and cortical areas of the right hemisphere of the brain, and once encoded leave a lasting blueprint for affect regulation, cognitive expectations, and behavior in later relationships. Their research interest in how attachment experiences affect brain activity has further substantiated the relevance of a child's relationships on development as well as elucidating that "bodily experience" (Holmes, 2007) is part of mental life. From the first weeks and months of life, when attachment needs are mainly expressed as body-based needs and much communication between newborn and parent is through touch, the quality of their physical and emotional interactions is being laid down in the pathways and connections of the baby's brain (Ogden, Minton, & Pain, 2006; Stauffer, 2009).

Citing Freud's phrase "the ego is first and foremost a bodily ego" as an example, Diamond (2003) asserts that attachment theory's model of psychobiological development brings the body back to psychoanalysis. What the theory adds to psychoanalytic thought, however, is that the body develops through key relationships (Orbach, 2004). Optimal attachment experiences that promote secure attachment and resilience are, therefore, both a psychological and physical achievement (Ogden et al., 2006). Moreover, Schore (2001) alleges that attachment experiences continue to influence brain–body processes into adulthood, a concept that has implications for the thesis that there is a system of attachment which remains active throughout life. The extension of the theory into adult attachment emphasizes that adults too require reliable affectional relationships that they can call upon for comfort or security when they are threatened, afraid, or lonely. Though there are different characteristics of adult bonds, the biological function remains the same: whether a child, adolescent, or adult, certain relationships are considered unique and irreplaceable, crucial to the person's emotional stability and physical well-being. Some attachment behavior, however, is directed to those seen as stronger, wiser, and older such as the child seeking a parent, while with others it tends to be flexible. In romantic attachments, for example, attachment behavior is generally reciprocal, with roles switching between seeking or giving care and support, and may also involve caregiving and sexual/reproductive systems (Mikulincer & Shaver, 2007; Sable, 2008).

Overall, adults do not tend to require the actual proximity that a young child might want for safety or support, but they need to know they have someone who is looking out for them and keeps track of their whereabouts (Sable, 2008). Adults also have a memory network of internalized representations of their relationships that they can call upon to evaluate a situation, soothe distress, or bolster their self-esteem. These mental representations, or "working models" (Bowlby, 1973), composed of both conscious and unconscious elements, are perceived to be adjustable, adaptive mechanisms for processing information about the environment as well as the person's own internal state.

The following quotation from Bowlby's (1975) discussion of a paper by Stoller illustrates his emphasis on the decisive effect of attachment on the development of these models:

> In my own thinking about personality development and functioning, I have found it useful to postulate that during childhood each of us builds up two working models, one of self and another of environment (especially of the significant people in it), on the basis of which we plan and act (pp. 252–253).

I choose this quotation because it is a concise statement of Bowlby's (1973) intention to convey that though working models develop out of interactions with a variety of systems, their foundation rests on two key features: whether attachment figures can be trusted to be available and responsive if needed and whether the person feels worthy of receiving their love and care. Developmentally, these complementary models are the roots of secure attachment and optimal functioning at any stage of life. Adults who grew up secure, or became secure as adults, have representations of themselves which make it easier to make and maintain close relationships, regulate their emotions, and engage in exploratory activities such as career opportunities, new friendships, and social interactions. Secure adults have an inner resource and resilience to think and talk about their experiences and appraise their problems and manage them with effective coping strategies. Along with an ability to rebound from adversity in a reasonably short time, they will turn to others for help and support when necessary, making them less likely to succumb to psychopathology (Collins, Guichard, & Ford, 2006; Shaver & Mikulincer, 2007).

From an attachment perspective, insecure attachment is seen as a risk factor for emotional problems and dysfunctional behavior (Shaver & Mikulincer, 2007; Sroufe, Egeland, & Carlson, 2005). It was Bowlby's (1973) foresight to recognize the enduring effects and clinical implications that defensive strategies of insecure attachment could have on an adult's affect regulation and ability to relate to others. He proposed that early troubling attachment experiences could be connected to adult attachment disorders, and he conceptualized these relationship ruptures in terms of separation or loss, or fear of separation. In psychoanalytic tradition, Bowlby (1973) tied childhood to adult distress while uniquely adding research data to highlight that real experiences, including attachment history together with environmental constraints, were related to psychological distress. As Bowlby (1973) put it, the direction that developmental pathways take, whether toward or away from mental health, reflects "an interaction between the organism as it has developed up to that moment and the environment in which it finds itself" (p. 364).

Separation

Bowlby's interest in the effects of real-life events on development started early in his professional career when he worked in a school for maladjusted boys. During his brief time there, he was struck by the severity of family disruptions in some of the children's histories and began to wonder why and how these disruptions could generate such emotional distress. Attachment theory was actually launched later when he decided to focus research on separation and loss and together with James Robertson, a social worker on one of his research teams at the Tavistock Clinic in London, used Robertson's films of children (ages 18 months to 4 years) going through separation from their parents to demonstrate the significance of attachment relationships (Kobak, 1999; Renn, 2007). Bowlby said he concentrated on separation because he wanted to call attention to a child's actual experiences, both present and past, to make it clear that the "environment really matters" (Senn, 1977). By showing that the children reacted with fear, anger, and desperate attempts to find their parents, Robertson and Bowlby (1952) were able to document that real-life experiences, such as separation, can threaten well-being.

In order to account for the processes involved, Robertson and Bowlby (1952) identified three phases in a child's reaction to separation: protest, despair, and detachment. Protest is characterized by crying, bursts of anger, fear, and distress, indicating an urgent and active attempt to search out and recover the missing parent. If proximity is not restored, there follows a phase of despair which is marked by a more subdued mood. The intensity of crying and physical movements is diminished and the child appears sad and withdrawn, as if mourning the loss of the attachment figure. In contrast to the protest phase when the heart rate accelerates, it now decreases. From an evolutionary perspective, reduced activity conserves energy, whether for a child who could become exhausted or an animal in the wild that must remain quiet and hidden from predators until its mother finds it (Hofer, 1995). In the final phase, detachment, the child again engages with others, but upon reunion with the caregiver behaves in an erratic way. Instead of excitement, the child may act disinterested or seem to not recognize the parent. Bromberg (2006) suggests that what Bowlby identified as detachment is a type of defensive dissociation which recent theorists, like Bowlby alleged, agree can persist, endangering later attachment relationships.

The evidence that the effects of separation, especially when it is prolonged or accompanied by inadequate substitute care, can persist, even into adulthood, was groundbreaking. Furthermore, subsequent research has substantiated Bowlby's belief that reactions to separation or fear of separation can occur and be traumatic at any age. Adults, however, have the ability to make cognitive appraisals of a situation, and Bowlby (1973) expanded his thesis on separation by saying that the expectation that an attachment figure would be available and responsive in times of danger or distress is a major factor in determining feelings of safety and security.

The idea that an adult's expectation of emotional availability is relevant to security draws attention to an essential aspect of attachment theory: the quality of current attachment relationships has a significant influence on a person's emotional state and behavior. Past experiences may bias how the present is perceived, but the reliability of ongoing affectional ties is a critical factor in determining whether an adult is secure, fearful, or depressed (Bowlby, 1973, 1980; Harris, 2004).

This criterion of emotional security has implications for both theory and clinical practice with adults. Psychoanalytic theory is extended to include current attachment interactions, and attachment-based psychoanalytic therapy weaves together a client's history of early trauma or pain with what is happening now in affectional relationships. Clients often come for therapy when they feel attachment figures are not available or responsive and will talk a great deal about their frustrated affectional needs (Harris, 1997; Sable, 1979). Freud (1926) too recognized that emotional distress was related to "the object" and in one of his later works defined anxiety as a reaction to the danger of losing the object; the pain of grief and mourning, a reaction to an actual loss; and defense, a process that protects the ego against instinctual demands that are threatening to overwhelm it. Bowlby (1973) built upon this outline when he connected protest (the initial response to separation) to separation anxiety, despair to loss, grief, and mourning, and detachment to defensive processes that deal with the pain of loss. Bowlby (1982) defined separation anxiety as "anxiety about losing or becoming separated from someone loved" (p. 670). It reflects our "basic human disposition" to respond with fear and anxiety "when an attachment figure cannot be found or when there is no confidence that an attachment figure will be available and responsive when desired" (Bowlby, 1973, p. 407).

For therapists working with adults, explaining the evolutionary significance of attachment can help clients understand the roots of the problems they could be having over affectional relationships. For example, because evolution wired us for attachment, it is adaptive to feel distress upon separation or threat of separation and to take measures to protect and maintain a bond. However, this lifelong tendency to respond to what Bowlby (1973) called a natural clue to potential danger (others, for example, include open spaces, heights, isolation) can be derailed by maladaptive circumstances such as environmental changes, emotional or physical abuse, and repeated experiences of separation or threats of abandonment, and the responses to natural clues become inhibited or intensified. From my experience as an attachment-oriented psychotherapist, I have found that encouraging clients to explore these unsettling experiences can help put them in perspective. Understanding that the evolutionary function of the attachment behavioral system is to assure connection can normalize how reactions are perceived, relieving the burden of shame and self-blame. Panksepp (2009) adds that as clients learn about these "ancient, inherited tools for living" (p. 5), they can deal better with upsetting feelings which in turn can lead to more positive emotional states. Noting that Freud too believed in "the biological foundations of the psyche" (p. 2), Panksepp (2009) uses evidence that we now have from both human and animal neurosciences to specify, for example, how responses to separation or loss reflect "ancestral neural codes" (p. 13), together with certain experiences which have shaped them. For example, the hormone oxytocin, associated with feeling calm and content, is released when we are in close contact with a comforting figure—whether a caregiver responding to a child's distress, the company of a cherished pet, or a therapist who has become a secure base for her client. Oxytocin can also be triggered by just thinking about an affectional relationship.

In contrast to this sense of comfort and well-being, threats to attachment security may produce stress hormones like cortisol which exacerbate distress, undermining both physical and mental health. By placing stressful attachment experiences in terms of the fear and anxiety of separation, or the sadness and grief of loss, Bowlby provided the context for understanding a variety of real experiences in a client's history of affectional interactions. Although it is not always easy to know when an actual or impending separation might turn out to be a complete loss, Bowlby built on earlier data from the separation observations of young children with findings from Marris's (1958) and Parkes's (1965, 1969) studies of adult bereavement to describe a grief process which not only pointed out the pain of an adult's loss of attachment but has become a yardstick for understanding grief and mourning.

Loss

In the third volume of his trilogy, *Loss*, Bowlby (1980) wrote, "loss of a loved person is one of the most intensely painful experiences any human being can suffer" (p. 7). It is noteworthy that the title of the chapter in which this quotation appears is "The Trauma of Loss," suggesting that Bowlby considered certain loss experiences so painful they could be conceptualized as a trauma. This was an innovative idea at that time since interest and literature on the concept of trauma was just beginning to get the attention of mental health professionals. We now know that loss of an attachment relationship can be traumatic, unleashing a physical and emotional upheaval of grief and mourning that lasts over a period of time, and can feel crushing and almost unbearable. Freud's (1917) introduction of the terms grief and mourning into the psychological literature, with grief defined as an intrapsychic process in which libido is withdrawn from the lost object, also noted this wrenching pain of loss, and he tried to explain how it could develop into pathological mourning, or melancholia.

Bowlby (1980) both extended and modified Freud's (1917, 1926) view with his definition of mourning as a "fairly wide array of psychological processes set in train by the loss of a loved person irrespective of their outcome" (p. 17). Like Freud, Bowlby (1980) perceived that the outcome could be healthy or pathological, and when pathological, there could be "scar tissue" (p. 22) from childhood that could lead to some degree of dysfunction in adult bereavement. Bowlby (1980), however, alleged that though he agreed with Freud's point that healthy mourning led to a change in the emotional investment in the lost person as well as a capacity to resume attachment relationships, "how we conceive…achieving this change…depends on how we conceptualize affectional bonds" (p. 25). In particular, Bowlby emphasized that the biological function of attachment is such that once a bond is formed, it resists being severed and may never be totally broken (Parkes, 2006). Therefore, initially upon loss, there is a strenuous effort to restore the relationship and this effort is only gradually and reluctantly given up. What a bereaved person really wants is to bring back the lost figure and this longing for recovery is reflected in Bowlby's (1980) outline of the mourning process.

Citing evidence from research, Bowlby (1980) described reactions as moving through a succession of four phases: following a brief phase of "numbing" where the person, feeling in a daze, is protected from registering an event that could become overwhelming, there is a phase of "yearning and searching" which is associated with an upsurge of attachment behavior and separation anxiety. From an evolutionary standpoint, these reactions can be understood as innately motivated efforts to regain attachments and may be manifested in eating and sleeping disturbances, anger, or sensing the presence of the lost person. The next two phases, "disorganization and despair" and "reorganization," are characterized by first a pervasive sadness as the bereaved begins to believe the figure will not be returning and then a resolution of grief with attachment behavior reorganized to include a symbolic connection to the lost figure along with realization that reunion is not possible. Although in normal grief, the person is able to accept the loss and resume daily activities, the process may take longer than once considered by traditional theory. For example, Parkes and Weiss's (1983) early studies found it may take 2 or 3 years to restructure working models, and in my study (Sable, 2000) of a normal population of women widowed 1–3 years, remarks such as "you never get over it, you learn to live with it" were common, suggesting that attachment behavior was not yet reorganized. However, I did find that by the end of the first year of bereavement, one can tell if grief seemed to be giving rise to a maladaptive outcome.

According to Bowlby (1980), there are two main forms of "disordered mourning," "chronic mourning" and "prolonged absence of conscious grieving" (p. 138)—absence is now generally called "delayed" or "inhibited" grief (Stroebe, Hansson, Stroebe, & Schut, 2001)—and he associated these atypical reactions with insecure attachment. Subsequent research on adult attachment has found hyperactivation of attachment behavior and chronic mourning in anxiously attached individuals. Though the evidence on deactivation and inhibited mourning in avoidant individuals is less pronounced, there are findings of anxiety and somatic symptoms which suggest there are heightened physiological reactions to their stress, possibly from shutting down access to thoughts and feelings of grief (Mikulincer & Shaver, 2007; Parkes, 2006). This was Bowlby's (1990) idea about Charles Darwin's 30 years of physical illness, anxiety, and depression, which he had been forced to suppress grief upon his mother's death when he was 8 years old.

In combination with one's attachment pattern or style, Bowlby (1980) believed that a variety of factors influenced the physical and psychological symptoms that characterize complicated grief. The nature of the lost relationship, including how important and central it was felt to be, also affects coping, with loss of spouse (or partner) generally considered the greatest risk for disordered mourning. This is the relationship that usually serves as the person's main attachment figure, and it is now well documented that there is a higher rate of mortality, injury, and illness during the first year of spousal bereavement (Gilbert, 2001; Hazan & Zeifman, 1999; Parkes, 2006). Other factors that may increase risk are circumstances leading up to loss and the loss itself, with sudden, unexpected, and untimely death, or violent death, more likely to lead to problems (Parkes, 2006). And, of relevance to social work's interest in systems theory, lack of a supportive social network such as friends and family also carries risk.

The painful "bodily rooted experience" (Fosha, Siegel, & Solomon, 2009) of grief is not the only challenge facing people who have lost a close affectional figure. Though not a part of grief, there are likely to be changes in their lives and/or family dynamics that could cause problems (Parkes, 2006). Clients may seek treatment for aspects of these other phenomena, only to reveal there is also a struggle over unresolved grief. On the other hand, there can be other kinds of losses and transitions such as immigration stresses or sudden physical disabilities that can elicit grief and motivate the need for therapy (Parkes, 2006). Included in an attachment-based therapist's assessment of a client's distress in these kinds of situations would be to consider whether symptoms reflect the function of an attachment behavioral system which may have been thrown off balance by certain problematic experiences.

Unfortunately, we are seeing momentous disruptions and shattered attachments in our present, post-9/11 world, a world where all of us, to some extent, have to integrate feelings of fear, insecurity, and lack of stability into our working models (Tosone, 2006). Reorganizing working models can be especially daunting and difficult for those directly involved in the dangers of war, and I use the example of working with military families to illustrate, as Basham (2008) alleges that application of "attachment-related themes" can assist couples who are suffering the effects of combat trauma. Basham writes that deployment(s) and combat stress can be understood as "disruptions of attachment" which place a burden on these families as they try to navigate the transition of reunion. Noting that multiple separations, fears of loss, followed by reunions can "overburden the attachment system," the goal of treatment is to help family members rebuild attachments. Briefly, Basham's technique is to focus on understanding attachment ruptures from the past, strengthen individuals' affect regulation, and assist them to reflect on feelings such as protest, anger, and grief over losses as they emerge in therapy sessions. With improved capacity to talk about and understand "the role of attachment processes" in their lives, these traumatized couples can begin to shift their attachment patterns toward a more secure future (Basham, 2008).

Concluding Comments

Bowlby's contention that evolution designed us to make and maintain lasting affectional bonds has given us a "new science of relationships" (Johnson, 2009), and we now have evidence from attachment-based research that attachment issues often contribute to the psychological problems of adults (Parkes, 2006). For example, Harris (1997) alleges that unmet instinctive needs for attachment are often what bring a person into therapy. According to Schore and Schore (2008), we also have findings from neuroscience which have increased clinicians' "awareness of real experiences," including how "the real relationships of the earliest stages of life," once encoded in the brain, are involved in regulating emotions and modulating stress into adult life. For example, they quote Watt (2003, p. 109) who wrote that "if children grow up with dominant experiences of separation, distress, fear and rage… they will go down a …pathogenic developmental pathway" (p. 12).

The advances in understanding how these kinds of experiences in the external world, both past and present, can impact internal representations give us a wider perspective on the origins of psychopathology as well as a compass for carrying out therapeutic change. Attachment-informed psychotherapy (Slade, 1999), derived from psychoanalysis and updated and expanded by research into attachment experiences, offers the experience of an attachment relationship as well as a framework for analyzing a client's life story and altering existing working models (Bettmann & Jasperson, 2010; Eagle & Wolitzky, 2009; Parkes, 2006; Schore & Schore, 2008). Schore (2009), for example, emphasizes the need to help clients improve their "emotional self-regulatory processes" by attending to the attachment injuries that have caused affect dysregulation. The springboard for this effort is to help clients feel safe enough to look at their attachment experiences, some of which will be distressing and painful.

Bowlby (1988) believed that the way experiences are described should be accepted and affirmed even if they are later seen in a new light. Fantasy and imagination are not necessarily discounted, but these too are perceived to be based on actual events

(Bowlby, 1988; Marrone & Cortina, 2003). Similarly, transference reactions are seen to stem from the working models that have been built over the years. As the source of these feelings and memories are explored and understood, clients come to recognize how the past is being represented in the present (Eagle & Wolitzky, 2009; Parkes, 2006; Sable, 1994). Holmes (1997, 2010) has pointed out that the therapy process itself is a microcosm of separation and loss with its inevitable constraints such as scheduled sessions, vacation breaks, and sometimes irreversible endings, and these can provide further opportunities to reflect on the impact of attachment events.

It was Bowlby's (1980) vision to discover that real-life experiences, which he put in the context of attachment, separation, and loss, are at the heart of our emotional and physical well-being. His attachment perspective has much to offer our psychotherapy practices in these challenging and unsettling times and seems to be increasingly useful to clinicians. It has become pivotal in the work being done on trauma, the brain, and psychotherapy. Attachment theory also offers practical implications for dealing with current societal concerns such as day care, family violence, and divorce.

We can no longer shut the real world out of our therapy sessions. Problems are too pressing, and fear and anxiety too pervasive. In order to illustrate the significance of this attachment viewpoint and to note there are a variety of attachment traumas that we may find in our clients, I conclude with a brief description of my work with a middle-aged woman, Katie, who came into therapy to focus on inconsolable grief over the death of her beloved dog, Joe. Divorced and living alone, Joe was her only companion and a source of her security for almost 10 years.

A key dynamic that I have found relevant in helping people deal with pet loss, and which proved to be a relief for Katie, was to explain and validate the depth of her distress as a natural response of grief when there is the loss of a loved figure, that is, an attachment bond. After a few months, when clients who have come for pet loss are generally ready to move on, Katie said she was better but "still not back to my old self." Along with her grief, we had discussed her early life, as well as her years as a single woman, her career opportunities, and her children who were grown and living out of the area. I encouraged her to trace back her experiences to see what we might have been missing, and one day she revealed that several months before her dog died and she began therapy, her son had been deployed to Iraq!

References

Ainsworth, M. D. S., Blehar, M. C., Waters, E., & Wall, S. (1978). *Patterns of attachment: Assessed in the strange situation and at home*. Hillsdale, NJ: Lawrence Erlbaum.

Basham, K. (2008). Homecoming as safe haven or the new front: Attachment and detachment in military couples. *Clinical Social Work Journal, 36*, 83–96.

Bettmann, J. E., & Jasperson, R. A. (2010). The integration of attachment and neurobiological research into clinical practice. *Clinical Social Work Journal, 38*, 98–119.

Bowlby, J. (1969). *Attachment and loss* (Attachment, Vol. 1). New York, NY: Basic Books.

Bowlby, J. (1973). *Attachment and loss* (Separation, Vol. 2). New York, NY: Basic Books.
Bowlby, J. (1975). Discussion of Robert Stoller's paper "Healthy parental influences on the earliest development of masculinity in baby boys". *The Psychoanalytic Forum, 5*, 252–254.
Bowlby, J. (1979). Psychoanalysis as art and science. *International Review of Psycho-Analysis, 6*, 3–14.
Bowlby, J. (1980). *Attachment and loss* (Loss, Vol. 3). New York, NY: Basic Books.
Bowlby, J. (1982). Attachment and loss: Retrospect and prospect. *American Journal of Orthopsychiatry, 52*, 664–678.
Bowlby, J. (1988). *A secure base*. New York, NY: Basic Books.
Bowlby, J. (1990). *Charles Darwin*. New York, NY: Norton.
Bromberg, P. M. (2006). *Awakening the dreamer*. Mahwah, NJ: The Analytic.
Collins, N. L., Guichard, A. C., & Ford, M. B. (2006). Responding to need in intimate relationships: Normative processes, and individual differences. In M. Mikulincer & G. S. Goodman (Eds.), *Dynamics of romantic love* (pp. 149–189). New York, NY: Guilford.
Crowell, J. A., Fraley, R. C., & Shaver, P. R. (1999). Measurement of individual differences in adolescent and adult attachment. In J. Cassidy & P. R. Shaver (Eds.), *Handbook of attachment: Theory, research, and clinical applications* (1st ed., pp. 434–465). New York, NY: Guilford.
Diamond, N. (2003). Attachment, trauma, and the body. In M. Cortina & M. Marrone (Eds.), *Attachment theory and the psychoanalytic process* (pp. 409–429). Philadelphia, PA: Whurr.
Eagle, M., & Wolitzky, D. L. (2009). Adult psychotherapy from the perspectives of attachment theory and psychoanalysis. In J. H. Obegi & E. Berant (Eds.), *Attachment theory and research in clinical work with adults* (pp. 351–378). New York, NY: Guilford.
Fonagy, P. (2001). *Attachment theory and psychoanalysis*. New York, NY: Other.
Fosha, D., Siegel, D. J., & Solomon, M. F. (2009). Introduction. In D. Fosha, D. J. Siegel, & M. Solomon (Eds.), *The healing power of emotion (VII–XIII)*. New York, NY: W.W. Norton.
Freud, S. (1917). Mourning and melancholia. *Standard Edition, 14*, 239–258.
Freud, S. (1926). Inhibitions, symptoms and anxiety. *Standard Edition, 20*, 75–175.
Gilbert, P. (2001). Evolutionary approaches to psychopathology: The role of natural defenses. *Australian and New Zealand Journal of Psychiatry, 35*, 17–27.
Goldstein, E. G. (2009). The relationship between social work and psychoanalysis: The future of social workers. *Clinical Social Work Journal, 37*, 7–13.
Harris, T. (1997). Adult attachment processes and psychotherapy: A commentary on Bartholomew and Birtchnell. *British Journal of Medical Psychology, 70*, 281–290.
Harris, T. (2004). Chef or chemist? Practicing psychotherapy within the attachment paradigm. *Attachment and Human Development, 6*, 191–207.
Hazan, C., & Zeifman, D. (1999). Pair bonds as attachments: Evaluating the evidence. In J. Cassidy & P. R. Shaver (Eds.), *Handbook of attachment: Theory, research and clinical applications* (pp. 336–354). New York, NY: Guilford.
Hofer, M. A. (1995). Hidden regulators: Implications for a new understanding of attachment, separation and loss. In S. Goldberg, R. Muir, & J. Kerr (Eds.), *Attachment theory, social, developmental, and clinical perspectives* (pp. 203–230). Hillsdale, NJ: Analytic.
Holmes, J. (1997). *Attachment, intimacy, autonomy: Using attachment theory in adult psychotherapy*. Northvale, NJ: Jason Aronson.
Holmes, J. (2007). Sex, couples, and attachment: The role of hedonic intersubjectivity. *Attachment: New Directions in Psychotherapy and Relational Psychoanalysis, 2*, 18–29.
Holmes, J. (2010). *Exploring in security: Towards an attachment-informed psychoanalytic psychotherapy*. London, England: Routledge.
Johnson, S. (2009). Extravagant emotion: Understanding and transforming love relationships in emotionally focused therapy. In D. Fosha, D. J. Siegel, & M. Solomon (Eds.), *The healing power of emotion* (pp. 257–279). New York, NY: W.W. Norton.
Kobak, R. (1999). The emotional dynamics of disruptions in attachment relationships: Implications for theory, research, and clinical intervention. In J. Cassidy & P. R. Shaver (Eds.), *Handbook of attachment: Theory, research and clinical applications* (1st ed., pp. 21–43). New York, NY: Guilford.

Kraemer, G. W., Lamb, M. E., Liotti, G. A., Lyons-Ruth, K., Meinlschmidt, G., Scholmerich, A., Steele, M., & Travarthen, C. (2005). Group report: Adaptive and maladaptive outcomes. In C. S. Carter, L. Ahnert, K. E. Grossman, S. B. Hrdy, M. E. Lamb, S. W. Ponges, & N. Sachser (Eds.), *Attachment and bonding: A new synthesis* (pp. 429–474). Cambridge, MA: MIT Press.

Marris, P. (1958). *Widows and their families*. London, England: Routledge.

Marrone, M., & Cortina, M. (2003). Introduction: Reclaiming Bowlby's contribution to psychoanalysis. In M. Cortina & M. Marrone (Eds.), *Attachment theory and the psychoanalytic process* (pp. 1–24). London, England: Whurr.

Mikulincer, M., & Shaver, P. R. (2007). *Attachment in adulthood: Structure, dynamics and change*. New York, NY: Guilford.

Ogden, P., Minton, K., & Pain, C. (2006). *Trauma and the body: A sensorimotor approach to psychotherapy*. New York, NY: W.W. Norton.

Orbach, S. (2004). What can we learn from them? *Attachment and Human Development, 6*, 141–150.

Panksepp, J. (2009). Brain emotional systems and qualities of mental life: From animal models of affect to implications for psychotherapeutics. In D. Fosha, D. J. Siegel, & M. Solomon (Eds.), *The healing power of emotion* (pp. 1–26). New York, NY: W.W. Norton & Co.

Parkes, C. M. (1965). Bereavement and mental illness. *British Journal of Medical Psychology, 38*, 1–26.

Parkes, C. M. (1969). Separation anxiety: An aspect of the search for a lost object. In M. H. Lader (Ed.), *British Journal of Psychiatry Special Publication, No. 3: Studies of Anxiety* (pp. 87–92). London, England: World Psychiatric Association and the Royal Medico-Psychological Association.

Parkes, C. M. (2006). *Love and loss*. London, England: Routledge.

Parkes, C. M., & Weiss, R. S. (1983). *Recovery from bereavement*. New York, NY: Basic Books.

Reeves, R. (2008). Breaking free from Procrustean orthodoxy: Personal reflections after the 2007 Bowlby Memorial conference. *Attachment: New Directions in Psychotherapy and Relational Psychoanalysis, 2*, 108–113.

Renn, P. (2007). Stop thief! But what has been stolen and by whom? Discussion of paper by John Bowlby. *Attachment: New Directions in Psychotherapy and Relational Psychoanalysis, 1*, 71–77.

Robertson, J., & Bowlby, J. (1952). Responses of young children to separation from their mothers. *Courier, Centre International de l'Enfance, II*, 131–142.

Sable, P. (1979). Differentiating between attachment and dependency in theory and practice. *Social Casework, 60*, 138–144.

Sable, P. (1994). Attachment, working models, and real experiences. *Journal of Social Work Practice, 8*, 25–34.

Sable, P. (2000). *Attachment and adult psychotherapy*. Northvale, NJ: Jason Aronson.

Sable, P. (2008). What is adult attachment? *Clinical Social Work Journal, 36*, 21–30.

Sable, P. (2010). The origins of an attachment approach to social work. In S. Bennett, & J.K. Nelson (Eds.), Adult attachment in clinical social work (pp.17–29). New York, NY: Springer.

Schore, A. N. (1994). *Affect regulation and the origin of the self: The neurobiology of emotional development*. Hillsdale, NJ: Erlbaum.

Schore, A. N. (1997). A century after Freud's Project: Is a rapprochement between psychoanalysis and neurobiology at hand? *Journal of the American Psychoanalytic Association, 45*, 841–867.

Schore, A. N. (1999). Commentary on emotions: Neuropsychoanalytic views. *Neuropsychoanalysis, 1*, 49–55.

Schore, A.N. (2001). Minds in the making: Attachment, the self-organizing brain, and developmentally-oriented psychoanalytic psychotherapy. *British Journal of Psychotherapy, 17*, 299–328.

Schore, A. N. (2003a). *Affect dysregulation and disorders of the self*. New York, NY: W.W. Norton.

Schore, A. N. (2003b). *Affect regulation and the repair of the self*. New York, NY: W.W. Norton.

Schore, A. N. (2009). Right brain affect regulation: an essential mechanism of development, trauma, dissociation, and psychotherapy. In D. Fosha, D. Siegel, & M. Solomon (Eds), *The healing power of emotion: Affective neuroscience, development, & clinical practice* (pp. 112–144). New York: W. W. Norton.

Schore, J. R., & Schore, A. N. (2008). Modern attachment theory: The central role of affect regulation in development and treatment. *Clinical Social Work Journal, 36*, 9–20.

Schwartz, J. (2007). Editorial. *Attachment: New Directions in Psychotherapy and Relational Psychoanalysis, 1*, VII–XII.

Schwartz, J. (2008). Why attachment theory is a better theory and why no one wants it. *Attachment: New Directions in Psychotherapy and Relational Psychoanalysis, 2*, 150–158.

Senn, M. J. E. (1977). Interview with John Bowlby. In M. J. E. Senn (Ed.), *Milton J.E. Senn oral history collection: History of medicine division*. Washington, DC: National Library of Medicine.

Shaver, P. R., & Mikulincer, M. (2007). Adult attachment theory and the regulation of emotion. In J. J. Gross (Ed.), *Handbook of emotional regulation* (pp. 446–465). New York, NY: Guilford.

Siegel, D. J. (1999). *The developing mind: Toward a neurobiology of interpersonal experience*. New York, NY: Guilford.

Slade, A. (1999). Attachment theory and research: Implications for the theory and practice of individual psychotherapy with adults. In J. Cassidy & P. R. Shaver (Eds.), *Handbook of attachment: Theory, research and clinical applications* (1st ed., pp. 575–594). New York, NY: Guilford.

Sroufe, L. A., & Waters, E. (1977). Attachment as an organizational construct. *Child Development, 48*, 1184–1199.

Sroufe, L. A., Egeland, B., & Carlson, E. (2005). Placing early attachment experiences in developmental context: The Minnesota longitudinal study. In K. E. Grossman, K. Grossman, & E. Waters (Eds.), *Attachment from infancy to adulthood: The major longitudinal studies* (pp. 48–70). New York, NY: Guilford.

Stauffer, K. (2009). Self-regulation: The ways of nature. *Attachment: New Directions in Psychotherapy and Relational Psychoanalysis, 3*, 30–37.

Stone, L. (1954). The widening scope of indications for psychoanalysis. *Journal of the American Psychoanalytic Association, 2*, 567–594.

Stroebe, M., Hansson, R. O., Stroebe, W., & Schut, H. A. W. (Eds.). (2001). *Handbook of bereavement research: Consequences, coping, and care*. Washington, DC: American Psychological Association.

Tosone, C. (2006). Therapeutic Intimacy: A post-9/11 perspective. *Smith College Studies in Social Work, 76*(4), 89–98.

Watt, D. F. (2003). Psychotherapy in an age of neuroscience: Bridges to affective neuroscience. In J. Corrigall & H. Wilkinson (Eds.), *Revolutionary connections. Psychotherapy and neuroscience* (pp.79–115). Karmac: London.

White, K., & Schwartz, J. (2007). Attachment here and now: An interview with Peter Fonagy. *Attachment: New Directions in Psychotherapy and Relational Psychoanalysis, 1*, 57–61.

Chapter 10
Saving the World One Patient at a Time: Psychoanalysis and Social Critique

Jennifer Tolleson

The heart of psychoanalytic thought is critique

(Kovel, 1976, p. 171)

There has been a stunning reticence in the psychoanalytic psychotherapeutic world to engage in vigorous critique of the larger social world and our place within it.[1] Our participation in dominant social processes, including the degree to which we are authorized by them, is distressing for most of us to consider (Cushman, 1994). Indeed, most psychoanalytic types are politically curious and left-leaning (while also tending to sequester our politics as private citizens from our clinical preoccupations[2]). But, of course, our professional values, theories, and methodologies, like every other cultural practice, are constituted by the matrices of power within which they operate. It is imperative, in our efforts to engage in socially responsible clinical practice, that we restore the sociocritical function to our professional mandate and that we apply such critique to our symbiosis with the dominant organizing social and economic order.

This article was previously published and is reprinted here at the permission Wiley-Blackwell (2009). Saving the world one patient at a time: Psychoanalysis and social critique. *Psychotherapy and Politics International*, 7(3), 190–205. Published online in Wiley InterScience (http://www.interscience.wiley.com) DOI: 10.1002/ppi.200.

[1] One could say that we, as psychoanalytic practitioners, have been negligent about engaging in collective protest about practices we know compromise our patients and our clinical values. There is a critical difference between private grumblings amongst ourselves and organized mass action.

[2] I am interested in the split between personal politics and professional practice, especially among psychoanalytic social workers. Many social workers began their careers with a keen interest in social justice and grassroots helping methodologies. In moving towards psychoanalysis (moving right?), many of us feel that we have left something of ourselves behind.

J. Tolleson (✉)
Smith College, Institute for Clinical Social Work, Burlington, Vt. 05401, USA
e-mail: Jentolleson@comcast.net

E. Ruderman and C. Tosone (eds.), *Contemporary Clinical Practice: The Holding Environment Under Assault*, Essential Clinical Social Work Series,
DOI 10.1007/978-1-4614-4124-3_10, © Springer Science+Business Media New York 2013

Wachtel (2002) writes that in contrast to its revolutionary origins, psychoanalysis has become an "establishment profession that fits easily into the practices and social structure of our highly unequal society" (p. 199). With all of the potency and critical depth of the psychoanalytic paradigm, we are strangely silent about the radical inequities that pervade American life. Instead, we tend to confine our observations largely to the private—or domestic—sphere. So while we have, for instance, much to say about parental failure, we are nearly silent about the failure of our (all too human) government to provide a living wage or basic health care to its citizens. We have a lot to say about the sources and problematics of human violence as it occurs between individuals and inside families but almost no critique of state-sponsored violence, as in, for example, the death penalty, the so-called war on terror, including the use of torture, the practice of extraordinary rendition, and the United States funding of military occupations abroad. We have a lot to say about mania, greed, and emptiness but are nearly silent on the homogenization of American life, its rabid consumerism, and uncritical submission to the logic of the marketplace.

Perhaps we have accepted our place in the continua of human knowledge and have dutifully left the meta-analyses to economists, sociologists, and political theorists; perhaps we are beaten down by years of battling a culture that burns our books, finds our ideas speculative and insufficiently empirical, and prefers the mania of the quick fix to the more sobering and formidable process of self-inquiry; perhaps we are anxious about risking the mainstream acceptance we have achieved over time.

Whatever the case, the radical deconstructive spirit has gone largely AWOL in this profession of ours, our heads too often in the sand about the larger sociohistorical contexts and political/economic practices that structure our patients' lives, our theories and methodologies, and our collective professional values. We do not address social inequities as much as perform them, doing so in the nuance of enactment with our patients (Layton, 2005), in the social reifications of our theories,[3] in our neglect of cultural history in our clinical work, and in the unexamined alliances we make with those who fund our services.

In the headlong rush to achieve credibility in the mainstream, to satisfy the demands of the marketplace, and to fit in, we have become participants (and unwitting collaborators) in a system we might otherwise challenge.[4] If psychoanalysis was once part of a countercultural critique, calling into question the organizing social practices of the day, one could argue that we have long since learned to keep our mouths shut. It may be that many practitioners have replaced activist efforts in the social world with creating "the good society" in the intimacies of the therapeutic dyad. Doing psychotherapy, with its contemporary democratizing thrust (i.e., empathy, mutuality, antiauthoritarianism), provides possibilities for clinicians to fashion a social utopia in

[3] By "reification," I mean treating what is essentially ideological, or socially/culturally produced, as the natural order of things.

[4] This is blatant in the realms of managed care, diagnosis and medicalization, and so-called evidence-based practice (see Gourguechon (2007), Pyles (2003), Scholom (1998), and Walls (2004, 2006, 2007), for critiques on the takeover of psychoanalysis by corporatized health care and scientism).

the privacies of their work (Boticelli, 2004; Gordon, 1995) in lieu of social action on the streets. Importantly, in a century that has seen family and communal dependencies diluted by suburbanization, the demands of industrialization, and the waning of traditional binding practices (like religion and the family dinner), psychotherapy has been something of a refuge, providing people with intimate, empathic human contact (Cushman, 1995). Problematically, however, "our patients come to therapy rather than form social alliances and rebel" (Layton, 2004, p. 243), rendering psychotherapy a soothing and compensatory healing accommodation rather than a viable challenge to the sources of alienation in our patient's lives. Like a Mother who comforts her child after he has endured a beating by his father, we help our patients feel better but stop short of confrontation with the system. Referring to managed care as a "source of dehumanization," Boticelli (2004) decries the absence of mass political action on the part of clinicians:

> Instead of calling for the creation of a movement that could directly challenge the right of insurance companies to profit by denying the health care that they are mandated to provide, [it is suggested]... that researchers conduct outcome studies to demonstrate the cost-effectiveness of psychoanalytic therapy, in the hope that this data will convince insurance companies to pay for it. (p. 644)

Employing a strategy of accommodation, we wind up doing treatment (or research) in lieu of social praxis, fitting in instead of talking back.

But this was not always the case. At varying points along the way, and in differing regions of the world, psychoanalysis has served as a progressive social philosophy alongside its application as a psychological treatment.[5] Freud (1926) himself believed that the greatest contribution of the psychoanalytic project lay in its power as a social transformational discourse and that its utility as a form of clinical treatment would be secondary.[6] Our clinical work, he suggested about himself, earns us a living, while we are otherwise changing the world. The revolutionary potency of the psychoanalytic discourse lay, at its best, in its de facto challenge and denunciation of received knowledge, its deconstruction of the illusions embedded in everyday life, and its (near heartless) refusal to take anything for granted, from the most sacred to the most banal.

That psychoanalysis has been historically regarded as a subversive project is evidenced by its violent exclusion by dictators and fascist regimes (Richter, 1996). In examining the dissociation of race from the psychoanalytic discourse, Altman

---

[5] For a wonderful history of the social activism in the early psychoanalytic movement, see Danto (2005); for a compelling record of the social emancipatory work of Marie Langer and her fellow radical analysts in Latin America, see Hollander (1997).

[6] Freud, in *The Question of Lay Analysis* (1926), wrote, "For we do not consider it at all desirable for psycho-analysis to be swallowed up by medicine and to find its last resting place in a text book of psychiatry under the heading 'Methods of Treatment'... As a depth psychology, a theory of the mental unconscious, it can become indispensable to all the sciences, which are concerned with the evolution of human civilization and its major institutions such as art, religion and social order... The use of analysis for the treatment of neurosis is only one of its applications; the future will perhaps show that it is not the most important one. It would be wrong to sacrifice all the other applications to this single one" (p. 248).

(2004) writes that at its inception, psychoanalysis was "a black thing," based on the high affiliation of Jews, who were referred to as "black" in Vienna (Gilman, in Altman, 2004) at that time. This racialization of psychoanalysis, the ongoing anti-Semitic assaults against it, the repudiation of its emphasis on desire and death, and the socialist and communist affiliations of so many of its early practitioners placed psychoanalysis, in its beginnings, firmly in the social margins. Comprised of people who were social reformers, political radicals, medical mavericks, and humanitarians, people who broke ranks with tradition, like women and Marxists (Jacoby, 1983), the early psychoanalytic movement, one could say, occupied a subject position that stood in opposition to—if not defiance of—mainstream culture. This position simultaneously required and inspired a creativity of mind, an independence of purpose, and the sort of critical scrutiny of the dominant surround that is only possible when one is standing outside it.

Necessarily, psychoanalysis depoliticized during the Nazi period. In mortal danger, practitioners fled for their lives, many to the USA. Altman (2004) writes that once safely here these refugees "…sought (consciously or unconsciously) to join the ranks of white Americans… to adopt unreflectively a Northern European value system and to seek upper class social status" (p. 808). This identification with whiteness (as a social construction and subject position) joined them to the wheels of capitalism, which included medicalizing and privatizing. Ego psychology, with its emphasis on adaptation, frustration tolerance, and the stiff upper lip, became the chief operating theory. In addition, the degradations brought about by the relocation of psychoanalysis to America, that is, its anti-intellectualism,[7] its antagonism toward Marxism, and its rejection of lay practitioners (furthering medicalization), "conspired," writes Jacoby (1983), " to domesticate psychoanalysis, subduing its broader and…critical implications" (p. 17).

As it Americanized over time,[8] the profession's notion of itself as apolitical became a proud part of its working value system. According to Richter (1996),

[7] Arguably, American anti-intellectualism continues to thwart a meaningful public role for a psychoanalytic discourse. For Gordon (1995), psychoanalysis as a discipline has failed to contribute to public intellectual conversation and has become increasingly insular and cut off from the public sphere: "Indeed, on the contrary, it has produced a rather self-referential group of textual experts, talking to one another in an exclusive and rarified language about their own and others' texts… I could name hardly anyone in the field of psychoanalysis who could in any way be regard as a public intellectual, that is someone who seeks a mass audience outside of the academic world… The 'turn to psychoanalysis' taken by many leftists, feminists, and other radicals in the 1970s and 1980s has ended up as a retreat from collective engagement and a search for individual consolation in the self-contained politics of psychoanalytic theory in the academy" (p. 276). I would suggest that, contemporarily, Slavoj Zizek qualifies as a public intellectual speaking from the domain of psychoanalysis.

[8] Barratt (1985) asserts that the Americanization of psychoanalysis was an important factor in the loss of its sociocritical vision: "That psychoanalytic science is a critical praxis with inherently 'anthropological' implications is all too comfortably obscured by the American domestication of Freud's discipline….In the American setting the expansion of 'psychoanalysis' often seems to have depended on the occlusion of Freud's method as a unique mode of personal inquiry and change that necessarily issues into political and sociocultural critique" (pp. 437–438).

training programs in psychoanalysis began to seek particularly compliant candidates for its programs, preferring applicants who were politically conformist and rarely admitting those who would have been embraced in the early days of the movement: "...unconventional people, doubters... cranks, dreamers, and sensitive characters" (p. 298). There was a burgeoning of a Left psychoanalysis during the 1950s and 1960s, particularly among Marxist academics and socialist freedom movements that used the critical social analyses of the Frankfurt School to inform civil protest. But now Freud is dead, or so they say, and we could be (should be?), curiously, back to where we once belonged. This strikes me as an emancipation of sorts, an opportunity to reengage our work from the margins, which is where we do it best.

So there has been, over time, an abandonment of psychoanalysis as critical ideology and social movement in favor of its therapeutic function. Indeed, in the century since its inception, the potential of psychoanalytic thought to offer a subversive, even revolutionary, challenge to Western social values has been overtaken by its clinical application.[9] Increasingly, and perhaps especially in its American form (i.e., deriving from ego psychology), psychoanalysis has become, seemingly, more conservative in scope and tone, having abandoned many of its claims to social transformation and retracted much of its earlier political chutzpah. Whatever the case, clinical psychoanalysis has opted out of its contribution to critical social praxis and found safe harbor as an individual healing technology that promotes social adaptation rather than social unrest. It is meaningful that those who approach psychoanalytic philosophy as critical social theory are found largely outside of mainstream clinical practice, typically in the academic disciplines. It seems also meaningful that theorists who have used psychoanalytic thought on behalf of a radical social critique or sociological analysis have been marginalized or, in some cases, excluded from the therapeutic canon (clinicians in training, for instance, rarely encounter the theorists of the Frankfurt School), thus maintaining the functional splits between therapeutic practice versus social critique in the first instance, and between therapeutic practice as "colonial administration" (Kovel, 1988) versus therapeutic practice as cultural dispute in the second.

The absence of cultural dissent in the profession and the submission of clinical autonomy to the exigencies of the establishment have meant a tragic loss of vitality for the psychotherapeutic community (Richter, 1996). The "triumph of the therapeutic" (Reiff, 1966) in American life, the degree to which psychotherapy (as a cultural practice) has been absorbed comfortably into the cultural surround, rendered legitimate, has produced a waning of a particular sort of creative passion, a defensive smoothing away of dissent, leaving a banality where critique should be. Agreeing to our own corporatization, and sidestepping vigorous inquiry into matters as disparate and crucial to our integrity as diagnosis and the Mother/baby metaphor in treatment, we risk, quoting Cushman (1994), becoming "functionaries and apologists, chaplains

[9] Speaking to the surrender of the critical ethos of psychoanalysis to the clinical turn, Barratt (1985) writes, "... A technical preoccupation with the patient's 'cure' in an instrumentalist procedure that takes the givenness of things as its premise, results in a false cogency that conceals the political and sociocultural fabrication of the patient's characterology and symptomatology" (p. 438).

who *enable* the machine, rather than activists who *condemn* it and help others resist its march" (p. 805).

There exists a paucity of critical consciousness about the rootedness of our theoretical constructs in larger narratives of power, race, gender, class, and empire (Ghannam, 2005). The primacy of the Mother in our recent theorizing, for example, including the equation between doing psychotherapy and Mothering and the assumptions about what constitutes "Mothering" goes, too often, critically undeconstructed.[10] Simply, we too often mistake how things operate with what they are, confusing appearances for essences, and in the moment of our confusion, unwittingly reinscribe them. In the fetishization of the Mother in the theories of Winnicott, for instance, she—for Mother is always **she**—is shorn of her defining discursive contexts, as well as the social patterns that compose those contexts, including sexism, capitalism, and her place in those structures. "Mother" is reified, treated as a universalized "someone" responsible for the well-being of children in a particular, naturalized way, rather than understood as a social construct. Mother as constructed, then, becomes an organizing social discourse with which real women—and men—consciously or unconsciously must reckon. Addressing reification, Layton (2004) writes, "Discourses do not just describe; they have formative effects" (p. 242).[11] The psychoanalytic community has long understood the projective identificatory processes by which fantasy is realized and the Other is shaped.

If our unexamined and historically de-situated theoretical constructs reflect an unwitting alliance with the dominant social system, this is hardly truer than in the case of diagnosis. There are several recent texts that describe the making of the DSM (e.g., Kutchins & Kirk, 1997; Lane, 2007), revealing the farcical process by

[10] The psychoanalytic discourse on Mother, borrowing from and reinscribing the social discourse, is potent. Indeed, theorists as conceptually distinct as Klein and Kohut share in common the valorization of the Mother/child matrix. (According to Layton [1990], there is explicit male bias in Kohut's theorizing, as the responsibility for the mirror function is typically maternally assigned, while the father is more often the object of idealizing needs. Whatever bias exists in the theory also appears to correspond to a parallel bias in the application of the theory. In my experience listening to cases presented along self psychological lines, women therapists more often describe the transference of their patients in mirror terms, while men more typically speak of an idealizing transference. What is curious is how easily the gendered nature of these interpretive formulations escapes notice.) The Mother as an organizing *idea* in psychoanalytic theorizing goes, again, undeconstructed. A further aspect of the Mothering discourse in psychoanalysis is its application to particular theories of clinical technique, whereby the therapist is maternally conceptualized. Emerging from developmental models of therapeutic interaction that view the clinical dyad as a reconstituted Mother and child, the unacknowledged assumptions that inform our notions of "the good Mother," and what we, as clinicians, are reenacting in our efforts to be "good enough" require studious consideration. The equation between Mothering and clinical empathy or Mothering and a particular brand of benevolence (Tolleson, 2003) clearly needs to be examined. For Layton (2004), the premium on "niceness" and empathy in American therapeutic technique derives, in part, from white bourgeois ideals of femininity (which includes the disavowal of aggression and a tendency toward submission) and the feminization of the clinical professions in the past several decades. Again, without rigorous scrutiny of our working assumptions, we unwittingly perpetuate the very sources of psychic enslavement we hope to lessen.

[11] Brenda Solomon, a postmodern sociologist, puts it thus: "Ideas become real, in consequence" (2009, personal communication).

which disorders have been named, catalogued, and, at different points along the way, sponsored by "Big Pharma" (the pejorative nickname for the pharmaceutical industry). Much of psychoanalysis has been proudly suspicious of psychiatric diagnosis, yet there remains a keen attachment to particular descriptions of experience which are treated as a thing (e.g., borderline personality). Whether such labels are useful is less the issue here than the importance of our willingness to critique them as social constructs embedded in a cultural history that is raced, gendered, and informed by economics. In a curious twist, Bollas (2000), sharing a position with cultural critic Showalter (1997), postmodernizes the concept of hysteria by framing it as an unconscious performative pattern in which cultural narratives (like cutting, anorexia, multiple personality) are reified and reproduced, again suggesting the importance of considering the social and medical production of diagnosis. At its best, psychoanalytic psychotherapy deconstructs diagnostic lexicon rather than enacts it; at its worst, it degrades into "mere medicine" (Jacoby, 1975), in which practitioners treat "disorders" that have been labeled in a medically efficient nosology in order to justify particular medicines and treatments with the aim of moving the patient in culturally prescribed directions.

As psychoanalytic clinicians, we have tragically de-linked (Layton, 2006) the public and private spheres, severing the individual from his social world. Of course, Freud was concerned with the repudiated, the unknowable and unknown, the unspeakable and unspoken, with what has been refused from waking consciousness, rendered to the margins. And, of course, according to the psychoanalytic template, we are fundamentally composed, not simply by what we know but by what we cannot know, see, imagine, or represent. We are, in short, constituted by the missing. Psychoanalysis is distinctively organized around the vicissitudes of absence in the forming of human subjectivity and the centrality of restitution—and reclamation—in the clinical encounter.

If, as they say, "the personal is political," I want to argue here that what might be missing, absent, repudiated, unformulated in the human subject lies within the vagaries of our unarticulated political and cultural histories, histories rendered mute, trivialized, in part, by their taken for grantedness, their seeming banality in the course of our living them. As clinicians, we are sensitive to the transforming role of trauma and the pain suffered in the course of events that deviate from ordinary experience. We are perhaps less attuned to the tyranny of everyday practices, the hegemony of bourgeois culture, experienced unreflectively as "common sense," which accounts for the absence of social revolt among those who suffer most under its value system (Gramsci, 1971).

If we live something long enough, it becomes ordinary; it becomes nothing at all, equivalent to life itself.[12] Anthropologist Linger (1993) writes, "Common sense makes revolution hard to think" (p. 3). It is in the nature of the great civil rights revolutions that they have forced a radical critique of the ordinary working social order, a consciousness, as it were, of everyday life. It is revolution, in fact, that reveals the ideological structure of what has been experienced as the natural, inevitable order of things (i.e., common sense). Ideology is a notion that we typically

[12] Anna Freud (1967) said we are traumatized only by the unfamiliar.

reserve for the Other as a measure of his exoticism or his evil (for instance, in the USA, the Arab is ideological, while we ourselves are not, as we refuse to consider capitalism an ideology or type of totalitarianism[13]). Jacoby (1975) argues that our modern thinking on ideology pits it against "common sense and empiricism" and joins it only to rhetoric and theoretical abstractions that run counter to Western sensibility:

> The irony is that the Marxist notion of ideology was originally directed toward elucidating and articulating consciousness… [I]ts meaning [has been] repressed, and a conformist one, openly or implicitly celebrating the common sense of the 'West,' was introduced. (p. 7)

My Mother grew up in the segregated American South during the 1940s and 1950s. When I ask her about the apparent lack of protest by her and her otherwise well-meaning friends about realities as gruesome as separate bathrooms and dining halls, she explains that this was simply "the way things were." In other words, it did not occur to them to question it; nor did it occur to them to scrutinize other "facts of life," like the burgeoning American exceptionalism in the wake of WWII, or that being a girl meant aspiring to a husband and children; the evils of communism and the rightful buildup of an American nuclear arsenal; the ideals of heteronormativity and the "Standard North American Family" (Smith, 1993),[14] whereby, in the words of one child activist, "Daddy works, Mama cleans, Baby cries" (uttered, at 2 years old, as my first psychoanalytic interpretation, and equally, my first act of civil protest); and, more insidiously, the establishment of "the good Mother" as an organizing construct, represented by, and in turn animated by the work of Dr. Spock, among others, and the mounting intensity of the child abuse movement, which would have a huge impact on the shaping of guilt, sexuality, freedom, occupational power, and how maternal life could be imagined and resisted for my Mother's generation of American women. If my Mother had been in therapy during this time in history, might her analyst have helped her consider the larger shaping forces of her subjective life, her development not just within a family, but within a place and time in which particular discursive options, or grand narratives, were available for imagining a life? Might her analyst, furthermore, have helped her contest the limits of a discursive field rendered as common sense, to think beyond the borders of her own collusion with the prevailing order of the day, to undertake a resistance? We can hope.

Psychotherapy entails a critical reckoning with what is de-linked from the patient's lived subjectivity, including the "unthought known" (Bollas, 1985) of ideology masquerading as "the way things are." Psychotherapy problematizes everyday life (Smith, 1987). In this formation, the therapeutic process becomes

---

[13] Political philosopher, Sheldon Wolin (2008), uses the term "inverted totalitarianism" to describe America's (potential) system of power, referring to the domination of democratic institutions by economics. Unlike classic totalitarian systems, economic processes are not subordinated to politics; rather, politics serve the exigencies of capital.

[14] Dorothy Smith, a Canadian sociologist, uses "SNAF" to refer to how the discourse of the nuclear family organizes thought, talk, and self-experience, serving as a template against which (family) life is measured.

fundamentally deconstructive, political, and facilitative of a capacity for critical social awareness and resistance. Cushman (2005) writes, "…we live out the status quo until we begin educating ourselves. That is when a crucial aspect of becoming a human being begins" (p. 432). Psychotherapy, imagined thus, becomes a form of revolution whereby what has been unconscious (unformulated, repudiated) becomes part of a critical consciousness of the social world and one's place in it.[15] But just as the potency of political and cultural history can be disavowed from the patient's ongoing self sense, and just as his conformity to the dominant social order can persist without critique, the content of the clinician's own interpretive work can detach people from their broader social, historical, and political contexts, sponsoring a process that overly privatizes the dyad and celebrates the patient's bounded individuality. Kovel (1976) writes:

> Psychotherapists, consumed by the day-to-day task of helping the troubled, tend to forget that their work is historically situated and that it plays a very real, albeit ambiguous, social role. More exactly, they have not so much forgotten the sociohistorical side of psychology as much as failed to consider it in the first place. The forgetting is done for them by bourgeois culture, which established a split between subjective and objective realms, made a fetish of the former, and turned it over to psychology to 'cure' once the need for religion had been outgrown. (p. 171)

Psychotherapy (as a social practice) becomes, in some sense, adversative to social/political critique insofar as it engages the internal world and valorizes the inward turn (where reflection is praxis). One could argue that the psychoanalytic engagement of the psychological, the subjective, effectively services the demands of capitalism, doing so in multiple ways (1) employing soothing techniques that calm people down and quell dissent, softening what Gramsci (1971) called "the basic, negative, polemical attitude," or stirrings of class consciousness[16]; (2) reframing social problems in terms of individual psychopathology; (3) displacing blame for suffering onto local objects, like parents,[17] particularly Mothers, and away from larger constitutive structures. "In this gaze," writes Ingleby (1984), "every influence on socialization except that of the family is rendered invisible (p. 49)"; (4) reinscribing consumerism with developmental narratives about internalization and "the empty self" (Cushman, 1995); (5) tranquilizing human distress through pharmacology. Given the availability

[15] A difficulty of engaging a historically and politically sensitive therapeutic stance is the level of knowledge required by the clinician. Richardson and Zeddes (2004) wrote, "Mental health professionals are certainly not trained for such tasks. Indeed, they are indoctrinated, in the main, in…ahistorical modes of human functioning that actively impede their functioning in this way. Also, patients are perhaps decreasingly aware of…compelling moral ideals from their own cultural past or from elsewhere. Trying to broaden the dialogue could easily become the blind leading the blind" (p. 624).

[16] I would add to Gramsci's notion of the "basic, negative, polemical attitude" the stirrings of race consciousness, gender consciousness, heterosexism consciousness, or, in general, injustice consciousness. And I agree with Layton (2005) that facilitating this form of awareness is crucial in psychotherapy, not just among those who occupy these subject positions but among us all and that realizations along these lines, often enacted, will emerge in any mix-up of class, race, gender, and sexuality in the clinical dyad.

[17] This is what Deleuze and Guattari (1977) label the "mama–papa matrix."

and user-friendliness of the psychiatric discourse for articulating human pain (Hogget & Lousada, 1985), and the collusion of the therapeutic community with the aims of the pharmaceutical industry, the rampant medicalization of subjectivity is not surprising[18]; (6) reducing the work of psychotherapy to outcomes treated as commodities (e.g., higher self-esteem, better marriages, healthier children, and the like) rather than valued as a process with unknown—and perhaps zero—economic value; (7) essentializing narcissism. The kind of relational and expressional freedom celebrated implicitly in constructs like "self" and "authenticity" is an inherently conservative (i.e., freedom trumping equality) capitalist social ideal. To be sure, the privileging of narcissism intersects crucially with the commodification of the self in a corporate and advertising culture, valorizing the importance of self-expression, individual decoration, and uniqueness. So while we have fundamentalized narcissistic needs, and positioned ourselves clinically in relation to those needs, we have not done the same with morality needs—compassion, responsibility, caring for others (with the exception of Klein's essentializing of guilt and the pursuit of love over hate). Samuels (2004) criticizes the standard and reifying psychoanalytic theorizing in which the patient is viewed as an infant whose well-being rests on whether it is gratified or failed by the broader society-as-Mother. In a powerful reversal, he suggests we regard the patient as a "citizen" who is caregiver to the baby-world.

In sum, all of these trends help to produce subjectivities fit for American empire and a global marketplace. Certainly Foucault (1978) believed that the function of all social sciences is to promote the state's hegemony over its people. Kovel (1980) indicts directly what he calls the "mental health industry" for its effective social control. Cushman (2005) writes:

> ... a reason to work as a therapist is to help prepare patients to engage in effective progressive political activity... if our work isn't to prepare our patients to bring on and work toward a better world, what good is it (p. 440)?

To what extent can psychotherapy urge a critical engagement with the social surround? Disagreeing with both Marcuse (1955) and Jacoby (1975), who assert that the revolutionary goods are in the theory, not the practice, of psychoanalysis, Frosh (1986) argues that psychotherapy can be a powerful agent of social criticism and progressive political impact. Insofar as social processes do not affect subjectivity as much as constitute it, he argues, the therapeutic emphasis on the personal is also always a process of social deconstruction. The centrality of social structures, particularly capitalism, in the shaping of subjectivity was also emphasized in the work of Reich (1946). Cushman (1994) argues that in a hermeneutical paradigm, the psychological and political are not convincingly separate. And, of course, Samuels (2000) believes that the psychotherapeutic endeavor must involve meaningful

---

[18] On the issue of pharmacological treatment for emotional pain, Hogget and Lousada (1985) wrote, "We would not wish to dispute that in the short run this may help people, but it only does so by leaving their troubles untouched, by seducing them further with the 'ideology of management,' and only 'helps' by rendering their distress 'mute'... Distress is no longer clamorous, insisting, or improper; it has been made quiet" (p. 131).

exploration of the patient's political development. I would argue that the decision to interpretively disregard the potency of the broader social world in the forming of subjectivity, to expunge political meaning from the therapeutic discourse, is as political an act as otherwise.

Critical questions that organize psychoanalytic inquiry—Who am I? How did I get here? What's going on?—render therapeutic practice closer to a philosophical discourse than a medical discourse, to be sure. Yet helping people locate themselves as subjects, to find themselves in some meaningful way existing, not just within a specific family but within a much larger and more complex social and historical field is to help them reclaim disavowed informing narratives, or "subjugated knowledges" (Foucault, 1980), while also connecting them to the wider human community.[19] Of course, this sort of broader therapeutic inquiry requires a willingness on the part of the clinician to call into question the historical embeddedness and discursive nature of her own organizing constructs, and her unexamined collusions with dominant social discourses/ideologies which she treats as common sense (like, for instance, the centrality of the Mother in making sense of subjectivity and the validity of diagnostic lexicon). It requires, further, that she shift her curiosity from figure to ground, from trauma to the social ideologies that potentiate it (ideologies rendered "hard to think" by their ubiquity). It is so called "normal psychology" (i.e., common sense), and our collusion with it, that needs to be vigorously examined. Ingleby (1984) writes:

> ...the task for radical psychoanalysis is to show how crippling compulsions arise in the course of normal socialisation, and persist because they serve so well the maintenance of oppressive institutions... The development of a truly 'emancipatory' form of psychoanalysis...requires it's disembedding from the system of practices...within whose constraints it must remain an individualist, adaptationist, and essentially conservative form of praxis. (p. 60)

The work of mourning is at the heart of a revolutionary therapeutic practice. Mourning, says Butler (2003), as distinct from the narcissistic preoccupations of melancholia, politicizes the self by ushering one into a realization (a making real) of global suffering and its unequal distribution.[20] If the narcissism of the melancholic stance narrows the subject to the problematics of survival and self-care, mourning creatively broadens him to a compassion for others. "Then," writes Butler (2003), "[he] might critically evaluate and oppose the conditions under which certain human lives are more vulnerable than others, so that certain human lives are more grievable than others" (p. 16). The identification with human suffering, which entails a perspective on one's own suffering that situates it in a larger human discourse, brings one into contact with the Other as a living subject. It is my denial of the Other, he or she whose subjectivity I repudiate in favor of my own, that is the source of my own "beating heart" (Poe, 1966).

As clinicians, most of us had the experience of helping our patients sort through the agonies of 9/11. There was a collectively endowed space for the mourning of

[19] For Meyer (in Cushman, 1994), a psychotherapy that does not reckon with sociopolitical history risks "help[ing] the weak feel strong while remaining weak" (p. 822).

[20] Death, especially violent death, has always been decidedly racist (see Tolleson, 1997) and classist (see Goldscheider, 1971).

lives lost in the atrocities that day. My patients were much more silent on the ravages of Hurricane Katrina, and even more so during the recent—and ongoing—events in Gaza. Who counts? What matters? We tend to assign "trauma" to, or properly humanize, those whose subjectivities we recognize or that mirror our own, those who are given voice within our dominant political paradigms. Butler (2003) writes:

> … I am as much constituted by those I do grieve as by those whose deaths I disavow, whose nameless and faceless deaths form the melancholic background for my social world, if not my First Worldism. (p. 23)

What gets said and what remains silent in the clinical encounter, in this sense, reflects our social demarcations and stratifications, reconstituting the very balance of power that is the source of global suffering in the first place.[21]

If the human subject is formed as much by what we repudiate—by what we cannot or refuse to imagine—as by what we embrace, the encounter beyond the borders of our own knowing (a reckoning, one could say, with the denounced Other) becomes crucial to a complexification of the personal imaginary and a deepening of our humanity. Foucault (1980) was famously concerned with discourses that have been culturally submerged due to their critique of dominant Western paradigms. The desiccation of any knowledge that threatens the party line is analogous to how the human subject repudiates that which threatens his narcissistic equilibrium. Of course, the requirements of power (which is simply another way of thinking about narcissism) determine what can be thought, known, imagined, and felt. Power, via the ways it mediates culture, hence, sets the parameters for desire, for thought, and for language, determining who gets a voice and what matters (Cushman, 1995). Despite the relative absence of reflection within psychoanalysis on the constitutive role of gender, race, sexuality, economics, and nationality, the human subject is conditioned by the dynamics of power into which it is born. As such, the psyche is fundamentally political, discursive, and ordered according to the requirements of the dominant forming epistemologies. In contemporary Western life, one could say that the Corporation, shaping human desire and awareness to its own ends, "manufacturing our consent" (Lippman, 1922; Herman & Chomsky, 1988), sponsors us increasingly. Yet this reality seems to escape most of our clinical and metapsychological theorizing and seems rarely to enter our empathic or interpretive work with patients. Of course, our work thrives in a consumer culture—it is the air we breathe—which likely accounts for our disavowal of its significance.

That which is expunged from cultural thought and articulation—whatever does not satisfy the exigencies of power—is not demonized in the human subject as much as unformulated, not rejected as much as unseen. On considering the social inequality of death, Butler (2003) poses the questions, "Who counts as human? Whose lives count as lives? And, finally, what makes for a grievable life?" (p. 10).

[21] One facet of American life is the relative absence of contact with, much less apology for, the crimes of the state (like the travesties of slavery or military invasions against the Third World). I have often wondered if our culture's rampant consumerism is an effort to drown out a collective grief.

By marking certain graves and not others, the media spares us the complexities of free thought while producing and exoticizing the Other through his and her cancellation. Butler (2003) writes:

> There is no obituary for the war casualties that the United States inflicts, and there cannot be. If there were to be an obituary, there would have had to have been a life, a life worth noting, a life worth valuing and preserving, a life that qualifies for recognition...I think we have to ask, again and again, how the obituary functions as the instrument by which grievability is publicly demonstrated...we have to think of the obituary as an act of nation building... The queer lives that vanished on September 11 are not publicly welcomed in to the idea of national identity being built into the obituary pages. But this should come as no surprise, when we think about how few deaths from AIDS were publicly grievable losses, and how, for instance, the extensive deaths now taking place in Africa are also, in the media, unmarkable and ungrievable (p. 18).

It disturbs me that we rarely hear case presentations involving waitresses, truck drivers, migrant workers, and coal miners. It would seem we work for the —largely white—middle and upper classes, and we too rarely challenge this alliance. Those who practice on the ground, in community clinics, in rural or working class communities, or with the poor, do not, in the main, have a voice in the articulation of formal clinical theory.[22] Working from the margins, these clinicians have contact with our culture's hidden subjectivities, serving as witnesses of the radically discrepant distributions of justice in American life. These subjectivities, whose voices rarely enter our working consciousness, much less our journals, our conferences, our theories, and our practices, comprise hidden—subjugated—knowledges that remain, sadly, outside our formidable intelligence as a profession, exacerbating the split between knowledge in the grassroots and formal psychodynamic theory, and fomenting the long divide between the social justice arm of social work and the therapeutic mission of psychoanalytic practice. Aiello (2002), importantly, describes the absence of "representation in the symbolic register" (p. 4) for clients and therapists working on the margins. Solomon (2006) calls these underground discourses, often emerging from grassroots social work, "guilty knowledge," reflecting theorizing that is lived apart from the professionalizing—and sanctioning—stamp of formal theory.

In our close encounter with the tragedies and profundities of the human subject, we are uniquely poised to inhabit a critical, dissident, and ardent sensibility in relation to the larger political world. The immersion of practitioners in the subjectivity of individuals makes possible a compelling, provocative, and experience-informed perspective on the human subject in contemporary life, and yet our steadfast refusal (a refusal produced, too often, by our totemization of theories that delimit the therapeutic imagination) to look beyond the most proximal sources of human suffering (e.g., parental failure and the nuclear family) ultimately limits our social justice participation. So, too, does our preoccupation with holding onto our

---

[22] Arguably, our colleagues working in clinics and agencies too often cannot afford to attend conferences where we gather. They do not have a place at our table, nor do we, by virtue of being perceived as elite and having poorly articulated the relevance of our perspective to grassroots aims, have a place at theirs.

professional legitimacy, staying viable in the marketplace, which tempts us in morally dubious directions and dampens our freedom to elaborate a more oppositional, or dissident, sensibility. Butler (2003) queries, "What has happened to the value of critique as a democratic value?" (p. 21). To be sure, as clinicians, we support easily most democratic ideals, employing many of them studiously in the therapeutic situation, but what about the role of dissent? Or have we purchased (too much of) our professional security at the cost of (too much of) our professional integrity? To be sure, our "fear of falling" (Ehrenreich, 1989) structures and delimits what can be thought, felt, and articulated in the therapeutic process, as well as in our relation to the systems within which we work.

Our domestication, including our preoccupations with the pragmatics of practice, has entailed a critical loss of creative freedom. We risk a dangerous insularity insofar as we minimize our contact with other social science discourses (sociology, political theory, anthropology), occluding the vision of a psychoanalysis which might be at once more social and more critical. Confining fetishistically the interpretive field to infancy, the nuclear family circle, and to the transference, we are insufficiently attuned to the centrality of sociopolitical history in the shaping of the human subject and to political praxis in the healing of the human subject. Psychotherapy, as an emancipatory practice, might push beyond the terrain of emotional consolation, or political resignation (Marcuse, 1955), facilitating in the patient his own capacity for cultural dissent. Certainly the potency of reparation is well theorized in psychoanalysis and arguably the compassion engendered by mourning links the clinical project to a sociopolitical one. Samuels (2004) describes political action as "self-healing" in its own right.

We have to clean our own house, to take on our perspectival biases and limitations, and to restore history to our theorizing, critique to our praxis, and political resistance to our ethos. The categories we work by are always rooted in the social, historical, political, cultural facts on the ground, always revealing something of our private and collective interests. When we endow our constructs with the status of pure truth, when our ways of talking become naturalized, confused with "how things are," we descend into a culture of obedience, as thought gives way to conformity. Noting the hypocrisy of a profession that is concerned about human emotional and relational vitality but does little to fight government policies that hurt people, Boticelli (2004) suggests that a more politically engaged psychoanalysis, one that is confident in its ability to make a difference in the world would have less a need to prove itself, less a need to justify its existence by conforming it to a status quo we should be challenging.

Perhaps cleaning our house means, above all, examining our collective transference to the potency of the psychoanalytic discourse and the seductiveness of its clinical and conceptual ambition. Psychoanalysis articulates a radical, unsettling, and exquisitely beautiful view of the human subject. But psychoanalysis is only one way of thinking and talking about the human experience and its discontents, only one pathway to personal redemption. Perhaps our capacity for dissent emerges from our refusal to be in love with it.

References

Aiello, T. (2002, January). *From the margins: The origin of some relational concepts in psychoanalytic work in the inner city.* Paper presented at The International Association for Relational Psychoanalysis and Psychotherapy Conference, New York City, NY.

Altman, N. (2004). History repeats itself in transference: Countertransference. *Psychoanalytic Dialogues, 14*(6), 807–816.

Barratt, B. B. (1985). Psychoanalysis as critique of ideology. *Psychoanalytic Inquiry, 5*, 437–471.

Bollas, C. (1985). *The shadow of the object: Psychoanalysis of the unthought known.* New York, NY: Columbia University Press.

Bollas, C. (2000). *Hysteria.* London, England: Routledge.

Boticelli, S. (2004). The politics of relational psychoanalysis. *Psychoanalytic Dialogues, 14*(5), 635–648.

Butler, J. (2003). Violence, mourning, politics. *Studies in Gender & Sexuality, 4*(1), 9–38.

Cushman, P. (1994). Confronting Sullivan's spider—hermeneutics and the politics of therapy. *Contemporary Psychoanalysis, 30*, 800–845.

Cushman, P. (1995). *Constructing the self, constructing America* (p. 1995). Menlo Park, CA: Addison-Wesley.

Cushman, P. (2005). Clinical applications: A response to Layton. *Contemporary Psychoanalysis, 41*(3), 431–446.

Danto, E. A. (2005). *Freud's free clinics: Psychoanalysis and social justice, 1918–1938.* New York, NY: Columbia University Press.

Deleuze, G., & Guattari, F. (1977). *Anti-Oedipus.* New York, NY: Viking.

Ehrenreich, B. (1989). *The fear of falling: The inner life of the middle class.* New York, NY: Pantheon.

Foucault, M. (1978). *Discipline and punish: The birth of the prison.* New York, NY: Pantheon.

Foucault, M. (1980). In C. Gordon (Ed.), *Power-knowledge: Selected interviews and other writings, 1972–1977.* Hassocks, England: Harvester.

Freud, S. (1926). *The question of lay analysis. SE 20.* London, England: Hogarth.

Freud, A. (1967). Comments on trauma. In S. Furst (Ed.), *Psychic trauma* (pp. 235–245). New York, NY: Basic Books.

Frosh, S. (1986). Beyond the analytic attitude: Radical aims and psychoanalytic psychotherapy. *Free Associations, 1H*(7), 38–59.

Ghannam, J. (2005). The use of psychoanalytic constructs in the service of empire: Comment on Baruch. *Psychoanalytic Psychology, 22*(1), 135–139.

Goldscheider, C. (1971). The social inequality of death. In E. S. Schneidman (Ed.), *Death: Current perspectives* (pp. 34–39). Palo Alto, CA: Mayfield Publishing Co.

Gordon, P. (1995). Private practice, public life: Is a psychoanalytic politics possible? *Free Associations, 5C*(3), 275–289.

Gourguechon, P. (2007). *The canary in the coal mine: Psychoanalysis and health* (pp. 19–22). Spring: Psychologist-Psychoanalyst.

Gramsci, A. (1971). In Q. Hoare & G. N. Smith (Eds. & Trans.), *Selections from the prison notebooks.* New York, NY: International Publishers.

Herman, E. S., & Chomsky, N. (1988). *Manufacturing consent: The political economy of the mass media.* New York, NY: Pantheon Books.

Hogget, P., & Lousada, J. (1985). Therapeutic intervention in working class communities. *Free Associations, 1B*(1), 125–153.

Hollander, N. C. (1997). *Love in a time of hate: Liberation psychology in Latin America.* New Brunswick, NJ: Rutgers University Press.

Ingleby, D. (1984). The ambivalence of psychoanalysis. *Free Associations, 1A* (Pilot): 39–72.

Jacoby, R. (1975). *Social amnesia.* Boston, MA: Beacon.

Jacoby, R. (1983). *The repression of psychoanalysis: Otto Fenichel and the political Freudians*. New York, NY: Basic Books.
Kovel, J. (1976). Freud the revolutionary. *Psychoanalytic Review, 63*(2), 171–178.
Kovel, J. (1980). The American mental health industry. In D. Ingleby (Ed.), *Critical psychiatry* (pp. 72–101). New York, NY: Pantheon.
Kovel, J. (1988). *The radical spirit: Essays on psychoanalysis and society*. London, England: Free Association Books.
Kutchins, H., & Kirk, S. (1997). *Making us crazy: DSM: The psychiatric bible and the creation of mental disorders*. New York, NY: Free.
Lane, C. (2007). *Shyness: How normal behavior became a sickness*. New Haven, CT: Yale University Press.
Layton L. (1990). A Deconstruction of Kohut's concept of the self. Contemporary Psychoanalysis. 26:420–429.
Layton, L. (2004). Dreams of America/American dreams. *Psychoanalytic Dialogues, 14*(2), 233–255.
Layton, L. (2005). Notes toward a nonconformist clinical practice: Response to Philip Cushman's "Between arrogance and a dead-end: psychoanalysis and the Heidegger-Foucault dilemma". *Contemporary Psychoanalysis, 41*(3), 419–43.
Layton, L. (2006). Attacks on linking: The unconscious pull to dissociate individuals from their social context. In L. Layton, N. C. Hollander, & S. Gutwill (Eds.), *Psychoanalysis, class, and politics: Encounters in the clinical setting* (pp. 107–117). London, England: Routledge.
Linger, D. (1993). The hegemony of discontent. *American Ethnologist, 20*(1), 3–24.
Lippman, W. (1922). *Public opinion*. New York, NY: Harcourt, Brace.
Marcuse, H. (1955). *Eros and civilization*. Boston, NY: Beacon.
Poe, E. A. (1966). The tell-tale heart. In *The complete stories and poems of Edgar Allan Poe* (pp. 121–124). Garden City, NY: Doubleday
Pyles, R. L. (2003). The good fight: Psychoanalysis in the age of managed care. *Journal of the American Psychoanalytic Association, 51S*(S), 23–42.
Reich, W. (1946). In T. P. Wolfe (Trans.), *The mass psychology of fascism*. New York, NY: Orgone Institute Press.
Reiff, P. (1966). *The triumph of the therapeutic*. New York, NY: Harper.
Richardson, F. C., & Zeddes, T. J. (2004). Psychoanalysis and the good life. *Contemporary Psychoanalysis, 40*(4), 617–658.
Richter, H. (1996). Psychoanalysis and politics. *International Forum of Psychoanalysis, 5*(4), 295–301.
Samuels, A. (2000). *Politics on the couch: Citizenship and the internal life*. New York, NY: Other.
Samuels, A. (2004). Politics on the couch? Psychotherapy and society—some possibilities and some limitations. *Psychoanalytic Dialogues, 14*(6), 817–835.
Scholom, A. (1998). Managed care's assault on our hearts and minds. *Psychologist-Psychoanalyst, 18*(2), 6–12.
Showalter, E. (1997). *Hystories: Hysterical epidemics and modern media*. New York, NY: Columbia University Press.
Smith, D. (1987). *The everyday world as problematic: A feminist sociology*. Boston, MA: Northeastern University Press.
Smith, D. (1993). The standard North American family: SNAF as an ideological code. *Journal of Family Issues, 14*(2–3), 16.
Solomon, B. (2006). Taking "guilty knowledge" seriously: Theorizing, everyday inquiry, and action as "social caretaking". In S. L. Witkin & D. Saleebey (Eds.), *Social work dialogues: Transforming the canon in inquiry, practice, and education*. Alexandria, VA: The Council on Social Work Education.
Tolleson, J. (1997). Death and transformation: The reparative power of violence in the lives of black inner city gang members. *Smith College Studies in Social Work, 67*(3), 415–431.

Tolleson, J. (2003, June). *Narcissism, guilt, and the fear of the bad object: The therapist's personal anxieties and the perversion of clinical technique.* Presented at Being on the Inside: Case-Based Summer Series, Institute for Clinical Social Work, Chicago, IL.
Wachtel, P. L. (2002). Psychoanalysis and the disenfranchised: From therapy to justice. *Psychoanalytic Psychology, 19*(1), 199–216.
Walls, G. (2004). Toward a critical global psychoanalysis. *Psychoanalytic Dialogues, 14*, 605–634.
Walls, G. (2006). Meaning or medicine: The future of psychoanalysis in the professional schools. *Psychoanalytic Psychology, 23*, 654–660.
Walls, G. (2007, April). Diagnosis, epistemology, and politics: The PDM paradigm. In L. Aron (Chair) *The new psychodynamic diagnostic manual (PDM): How old is the wine; how new are the bottles?* Symposium presented at the Spring Meeting of Division 39 of the American Psychological Association, Toronto, Canada.
Wolin, S. (2008). *Democracy incorporated.* Princeton, NJ: Princeton University Press.

Index

A
Academic freedom, 62, 63, 65, 66, 69
Accreditation, 65, 66
Achilles, 37
ACT UP. *See* Aids Coalition to Unleash Power (ACT UP)
Addams, J., 13, 35
Adjuncts, 71
Adult attachment, 88, 89, 93
Aidells, A., 7
Aids Coalition to Unleash Power (ACT UP), 23, 24
Ainsworth, M.D.S., 86
Alexander, F., 35
Allderdice, T., 35, 39
Altman, N., 35, 101, 102
Anastas, J.W., 70
Animal studies, 86
Anxiety
  survival, 14
  unbearable, 14
Applegate, J., 13, 15
Applegate, J.S., 35–37
Attachment,2, 15, 19, 74, 84, 105,
  based research, 86, 94
  dismissing
  disorganization, 92
  experiences, 87–89, 91, 94
  figure, 21–23, 25, 26, 85, 88, 90, 93
  informed psychotherapy, 94
  insecure, 25, 89, 93
  preoccupied, 74
  secure, 85, 88, 89, 93
  systems, 26, 87, 94
  theory, 21, 85–90, 95
Auden, W.H., 29
Austin, L., 35

B
Balint, M., 35
Barish, S., 10
Barkin, L., 29
Barry, B., 32, 37
Begec, S., 19
Bender, C., 5, 51
Bereavement, 91–93
Bereavement, vicarious, 20
Berger, B., 5, 61
Bettelheim, 35,
Bion, W., 34, 76
Bloch, G.R., 29
Bloch, R., 29
Bollas, C., 35, 54, 105, 106
Bowlby, J., 21–24, 74, 85–87, 95
Brentano, F., 33

C
Capitalism, 31, 77, 78, 102, 104, 106–108
Caregiving system, 21, 26
Casework, 13, 29, 35, 36
Change agent, 29
Charity Organization Societies, 13, 35
Chochinov, H.M., 20
Civil Rights Act, 1964, 68
Clinical practice, 2, 14, 17, 33, 38, 70, 90, 99, 103
Code of ethics, 29, 52, 53, 58, 66–68
Columbine high school shootings, 20

E. Ruderman and C. Tosone (eds.), *Contemporary Clinical Practice: The Holding Environment Under Assault*, Essential Clinical Social Work Series,
DOI 10.1007/978-1-4614-4124-3, © Springer Science+Business Media New York 2013

Conrad, P., 34, 36
Conscious/Unconscious dialectic, 4, 14, 16, 17, 25, 29, 33, 35, 37–39, 46, 75, 76, 78, 82, 88, 93, 101, 102, 104–107, 111
Container, 53, 77, 80–82
Controversial discussions, 73
Council on Social Work Education (CSWE), 64, 66, 69–71
Countertransference, 1, 3–5, 7, 14, 22, 34, 37, 38, 41, 48
Crying, 22, 47, 87, 89
CSWE. *See* Council on Social Work Education (CSWE)
Cultural amnesia, 34
Culture, 2, 15, 16, 26, 35, 39, 46, 54, 61, 64, 65, 70, 73, 75, 77–80, 100, 102, 105, 107, 108, 110–112
Cushman, P., 77, 82, 99, 101, 103, 107–110

D

Danto, E., 33–36
Darwin, C., 93
Death, 6, 19–23, 25, 34, 38, 78, 81, 93, 95, 100, 102, 109–111
Deng, V.A., 34
Despair, 2, 19–26, 37, 89, 90, 92
Detachment, 21, 22, 89, 90
Deutsch, H., 35
Diplomacy, 16, 17, 38
Donald, A.D., 13
Dyck, G., 26

E

Earthquake, Haiti, 20
Eggers, D., 24
Ego psychology, 34, 35, 77, 79, 102, 103
Empathy, 3, 5–7, 25, 26, 32–33, 35, 36, 100, 104
Enlightenment, 30
Erikson, E., 35
Ethology, 86, 87
Evolution, 32, 78, 87, 90, 94, 101

F

Fairness, 32–33, 36, 37, 65
Fenichel, O., 35
Fraiberg, S., 36
Frame, 6, 39, 73, 78, 80, 81
Freud, S., 23, 92
Friendly visiting, 36
Fromm, E., 35

G

Germany, 75, 78
Gibbons, D., 16
Global compassion, 25
Global trauma intervention, 2, 19–26
Greater Good, 25
Greenson, R., 9
Grief, 2, 19–26, 90–95, 110
  adult, 22
  global, 20, 21, 24, 26
  infancy, 22
Grolnick, S., 29
Gutwill, S., 37

H

Hamilton, G., 35
Hartman, A., 63, 64
Health care, 1–7, 14, 17, 37, 79, 100, 101
  managed care, 5, 14, 100, 101
  commodification, 1–7, 14, 17, 37, 79, 100, 101
HIV/AIDS, 23–25
Hofer, M., 90
Holding environment, 2, 4, 13–17, 32, 35, 37–39, 53, 55, 82
Hollander, N.C., 37
Holocaust, 34, 74, 82
Homer, 9, 37
Homophobia, 16
Hull House, 35
Hurricane Katrina, 20, 78, 110
Hyde, C., 64, 65

I

Iliad, 37
Illuision of omnipotence, 14, 15
Industrial revolution, 31
Intolerance/tolerance, 63, 65, 69
Israel, 25, 38, 43, 73, 75, 76, 82

J

Jacobson, E., 35
James, C., 34, 37
Johnson, Y., 70, 71
Justice, 32, 33, 35–37, 63–69, 78, 99, 107, 111

K
Kant, I., 33
Kemp, S.P., 70
King, M.L., 10
Klein, M., 16, 35, 73, 74, 77
Kohut, H., 39, 77, 104
Kristeva, J., 35

L
Lacan, J., 35, 39
Langer, M., 35, 101
Layton, L., 37
Learned helplessness, 24
Leibniz, W., 33
Lichtenberg, P., 16
Lifton, R., 38
Lindy, J.D., 38
Locke, J., 30, 32
Longres, J.F., 64
Loss, 2, 3, 6, 8–10, 19–26, 29, 37, 51, 75, 78, 85–95, 102, 103, 112

M
Measterberger, W., 29
Media coverage, 14, 19
Michael Jackson's death, 20
Middle East, 3, 20, 76
Mikulincer, M., 23–26, 86–89, 93
Moses, R., 39
Munch, S., 70, 71

N
Narine, N., 19
NAS. *See* National Association of Scholars (NAS)
NASW Code of Ethics, 29, 58, 66–68
National Association of Scholars (NAS), 65–69
Natural clues, 91
Nava'i, Alisher, 26
Nelson, J., 2, 3
Nelson, J.K., 19, 21–23
Neuroscience, 86, 87, 91, 94

O
Obama, B., 17, 39, 64, 80
Object relations theory, 17, 34, 35, 87
Odyssey, 37
Oklahoma City bombing, 20
Open society, 32, 39

P
Panksepp, J., 91
Pappenheim, M., 33
Paranoid-schizoid position, 16, 38
Parkes, C.M., 91–95
Patriot Act, 4, 5, 51–59, 62
Pelton, L., 64, 68, 69
Perlman, H.H., 35
Piaget, J., 35
Play, 15, 25, 44, 54, 80, 107
Political correctness, 63, 64
Post traumatic stress disorder (PTSD), 9, 19–21, 54
  collective, 20
Potential space, 2, 13–17, 38
  collapse of, 2, 13–17
President Kennedy's death, 20
Princess Diana's death, 20
Professional, 6, 13, 14, 29, 35, 36, 38, 39, 42, 43, 45, 46, 52–54, 58, 59, 64–66, 68–71, 73, 75, 78, 79, 89, 92, 99, 100, 107, 111, 112
Projection, 16, 17, 35, 39, 80
Protest grief, 22
Psychoanalysis, 1, 3, 4, 6, 10, 17, 29, 32–36, 38, 39, 41, 42, 49, 73–75, 78, 79, 85, 86, 88, 94, 99–112
  applied, 17
PTSD. *See* Post Traumatic Stress Disorder (PTSD)

R
Racism, 16, 64, 67
Rangel, L., 39
Rawls, J., 32, 37
Real experiences, 9, 85–95
Reich, W., 35, 108
Reorganization, 3, 19–26, 92
  global, 2, 19–26
Reynolds, B., 35
Richmond, M., 35
Robinson, V., 35, 44
Ross, M.H., 17, 39
Ross, M.H., 17
Ruderman, E.G., 2–5
Ruth, B., 64, 65

S
Sable, P., 9, 86, 88, 90, 92, 95
Samuels, A., 39, 108, 112
Samuels, S., 9
Schore, A.N., 87, 88, 94

Schore, J.R., 94
Science daily, 19, 45
Scientist-practitioner, 71
Seidl, F., 70
The self, 9, 16, 20, 32, 52, 75, 77, 78, 80–82, 102, 108, 109
Self determination, 35, 52, 67
Self-object differentiation, 15
Self regulation of the market, 31
Separation, 3, 9, 15, 16, 21, 22, 74, 77, 81, 85–95
Settlement house movement, 13, 35
Sexism, 16, 104, 107
Shaver, P., 23–26
Shay, J., 9, 37
Shiell, T.C., 62, 69
Siegel, D.J., 87, 93
Simmel, G., 35
Simpson, G.A., 61
Smith, A., 31
Social action, 7, 10, 16, 17, 33, 101
Social action-activism, 14, 37, 101
Social change, 17, 23, 29–31, 33, 67
Social contract, 30, 32, 34
Social Darwinism, 31
Social democrats, 33, 34
Social fairness, 32
Social justice, 33, 35, 36, 63–69, 78, 99, 111
Soldier's Project, 39
Somers, M.R., 43
Speech codes, 62, 63
Splitting, 16, 36, 39, 81
Sroufe, L.A., 87, 89
Stern, R., 7
Strean, H., 9
Streb, M., 62, 67, 69
Stoesz, D., 65
Sullivan, H.S., 35, 77, 79

T
Taylor, C., 30, 44
Tenure/tenure track, 69–71
Terrorism, 14, 20, 23, 51, 54, 58, 59, 62
Thyer, B.A., 70
Tolleson, J., 10, 99, 104, 109
Tosone, C., 3, 41, 93
Towle, C., 35
Transference, 3–5, 14, 37, 38, 48, 76, 78, 80, 95, 104, 112
Transitional object, 15
Transitional phenomena, 15
Transitional process, 15, 16
Trauma, 2, 3, 9, 14, 16, 19–26, 33, 34, 37, 38, 74, 75, 79, 80, 85, 90, 91, 94, 95, 105, 109, 110
  collective, 20
  cumulative, 24
  global, 2, 19–26
Traumatogenic environment, 38
Trauma, vicarious, 20
Tsunami, Indonesia, 20
Twitter, 20, 41

U
Uelman, G., 63

V
van Beusekom, J., 16
Veil of ignorance, 32, 37
Veterans of combat, 19
Videka-Sherman, L., 70
Violence, 17, 20, 38, 39, 54, 75, 77, 81, 85, 95, 100
Violette, B., 7
Volkan, V., 17

W
War, 1, 2, 7–9, 16, 19, 20, 24, 30, 33, 34, 37–39, 43, 51, 54, 62, 69, 73–79, 82, 93, 100, 111
Weber, M., 31
Weeps, 22
Will, G., 66
Williams, J.C., 61
Winnicott, D., 13
Winnicott, D.W., 13–15
Wood, J., 19
Words, 6–8, 25, 41, 44, 48, 62, 63, 65, 75, 81, 106
Working models, 88, 92–94
World Trade Center, 20, 51

X
Xenophobia, 16

Y
YouTube, 20, 48

GPSR Compliance

The European Union's (EU) General Product Safety Regulation (GPSR) is a set of rules that requires consumer products to be safe and our obligations to ensure this.

If you have any concerns about our products, you can contact us on ProductSafety@springernature.com

In case Publisher is established outside the EU, the EU authorized representative is:

Springer Nature Customer Service Center GmbH
Europaplatz 3
69115 Heidelberg, Germany

Batch number: 10837190

Printed by Printforce, the Netherlands